Let Us Attend
A Journey through the Orthodox Divine Liturgy

by Father Lawrence Farley

Ancient Faith Publishing
Chesterton, Indiana

Let Us Attend:
A Journey through the Orthodox Divine Liturgy

Published by   Ancient Faith Publishing
                  P.O. Box 748
                  Chesterton, IN 46304

Printed in the United States of America

ISBN 10: 1-888212-87-X
ISBN 13: 978-1-888212-87-7

"The journey is to the Kingdom.
This is where we are going—not symbolically, but really."
—Fr. Alexander Schmemann, *For the Life of the World*

Dedicated to the memory of
Fr. Alexander Schmemann,
a voice crying in the wilderness.

Table of Contents

Introduction

The Importance of the Eucharist

I believe that participation in the eucharistic Divine Liturgy is the most important thing one can ever do. It characterizes, defines, and constitutes the true Christian, for the Christian Church has always determined and recognized her members, not so much by the private beliefs they hold about Jesus, but rather by the corporate and liturgical expression of those beliefs in the Eucharist. In the dark days of persecution when the Roman state waged war against the holy Church, the state did not forbid Christian belief—it forbade *attendance at the Christian Eucharist,* for in the Eucharist the Church recognized her own members. The Eucharist was everything.

Events have proven this ancient truth again in our time. During the time when the communist state persecuted the Church in the Soviet Union, the Soviet government forbade almost all forms and expressions of church life. But our communist foes made a single and fatal mistake: though they forbade the Church to do charitable work, to proselytize the young, to give private Bible instruction, they still (grudgingly) allowed the Church to perform the service of the Divine Liturgy. And this was the one thing needful (see Luke 10:42) for the Church to survive. In the Eucharist the Church found its sustaining life, enabling it to be the anvil that could wear out many hammers, the phoenix that could rise from the ashes of death.

The Eucharist reconstitutes us, week by week, as the Church of God, and nourishes us with His divine life. By *receiving* the Body of Christ, we *become* the Body of Christ. As St. Paul said, "We, *though many,* are one bread *and* one body; for we all partake of that one bread" (1 Cor. 10:17). That is, through our partaking of the one bread of the Eucharist, God makes us again into the one Body of the Church. The

Eucharist is therefore the sacrament of the Kingdom, the eschatological presence of Christ in this age. Through our participation in the Eucharist we belong to Christ, and, through Him, to the age to come. As the eschatological sacrament, the Eucharist takes us from this age and plants us, week by blessed week, in Christ, who has taken His throne beyond this age, at the right hand of God in the age to come (Col. 3:1). Of ourselves, apart from Christ, we belong only to the realities of this age: to our families, our clans, our tribes, our nations. Through our eucharistic inclusion and participation in Christ, we belong to this age no longer. Now we belong to Christ and to His Kingdom, to the age to come. The Eucharist makes us eschatological beings, men and women who have transcended this age, who have overcome the world (see John 16:33).

We find it difficult to live like this, to "become what we are." We need to recover an appreciation of the true meaning of the Eucharist: not simply as one among many of the so-called "means of grace," but as *the* sacrament of the Kingdom, the liturgical means whereby we remain in Christ and belong no longer to this world but to the Kingdom of God. The Eucharist is our weekly journey to the Kingdom. It does not merely *teach* these realities in (so-called) symbolic form. It *manifests* these realities. It really takes us, every Sunday morning, into the Kingdom of God, and brings us to a saving encounter with Christ, the One who *is* the Kingdom.

Unfortunately, many in the Church do not adequately understand this. They regard attendance at the Eucharist as only a helpful ritual, an inspiring Sunday morning interlude to aid them in their efforts to live an ethical life. They find the music uplifting, the words of the prayers (where audibly offered by the priest) edifying, and the sermon thought-provoking. And of course, participation in the Body and Blood of Christ provides "spiritual strength" for them to cope with the stresses and strains of trying to live like an individual Christian in today's challenging world.

It would be wrong to condemn such a well-intentioned approach. May God bless all acts of faithfulness to Him! If Christ rewards even a cup of cold water given in His name (Matt. 10:42), surely He will reward this also. But such an approach falls far short of the true significance of the Eucharist. The Eucharist is not simply one means of help among many for individual Christians. It is the means whereby God creates and reveals the Church in this age, the means whereby He plants His Kingdom in the midst of men, the place where all peoples of the world can find Christ in His fullness.

For the Church to fulfill her calling in these increasingly difficult and hostile days, we Christians must recover a proper and full understanding of the Eucharist. This book examines the portions of the Divine Liturgy one at a time, for each portion has its own history, and we must understand this history to appreciate how each portion contributes to the whole, bringing us closer to our liturgical goal. Thus, historical knowledge serves as the indispensable handmaiden to authentic contemporary liturgical practice. For us to experience Liturgy in the way the fathers intended (or rather, to do Liturgy in the way the fathers intended), we must know what we are doing and how the Liturgy developed.

I wrote this book for what liturgical writer Gregory Dix has called the *plebs sancta Dei*, the holy commoners of God, with the prayer that it might lead us all closer to the Lord Jesus through our fervent praying of the Divine Liturgy and increase our understanding of belonging, in Christ, to the age to come. The Lord Jesus saved us and gathered us from all the world into His Kingdom—from every nation and tribe and people and tongue—that we might stand together before His heavenly throne and cry, "Salvation *belongs* to our God who sits on the throne, and to the Lamb!" (Rev. 7:9–10). This will be our radiant and triumphal cry to ages of ages. By His grace, it is our triumphal cry even now in this age, as we stand together in the Divine Liturgy and offer Him eucharistic praise.

—Archpriest Lawrence R. Farley

Note: Throughout this book, I assume that a deacon is serving and so refer to the deacon's part, even though most parishes have no deacon and the priest must do these parts himself. Also, I use the Hebrew numbering for the psalms, so that (for example) the "shepherd psalm" would be Psalm 23, not Psalm 22, since this is the numbering system with which most people are familiar.

Chapter 1

Beginning
the Journey

When we come to the life-giving chalice on Sunday morning, we come in the totality of who we are and all that we have done. We stand at the chalice marked by the experiences of the past week—with all our sins, all our brokenness, all our ongoing struggles, all our spiritual victories. To experience the fullness of the Lord's saving presence at that holy moment and to find healing for our sinful brokenness and strength for future victories, we need to be fully there.

It is all too easy *not* to be fully there. We may arrive bodily at the chalice and still have our mind, our heart, our emotions, all our inner resources someplace else. For this reason, our Sunday morning journey to the chalice and to the Kingdom of God does not begin when we first enter the church temple. Rather, it begins the moment we arise from sleep that morning, before we leave our beds, wash ourselves, dress in our Sunday best, and drive to church. We must rise from bed anticipating our encounter with Christ, resolving to stand before the chalice with all our spiritual powers focused upon Him.

Our spiritual preparation is not just a matter of keeping certain disciplines, important as these are. Certainly, we must keep these disciplines: we must say the appointed precommunion prayers; we must spend Saturday evening in peace (no wild partying until two in the morning!), attending Great Vespers that evening if possible; we must fast from midnight. All this is true, but it does not get to the heart of the matter. For the heart of the matter has to do with *the heart*, that interior spring of motivation and longing. We must ask ourselves: Do we really want to meet God? Do we really want to be transformed—even if this is painful and involves change and inconvenience and loss? How badly do we long to meet Christ and be changed into His glorious image?

We may say that we want these things, but something lives in us that doesn't want them at all. Coming to the church temple is one thing, but meeting Christ in our interior temple and allowing Him to dismantle and change us is quite another. We find it easy to come to church, to sing along with the choir, to say the prayers—and still to remain inwardly "safe" and spiritually withdrawn from Christ, determined not to depart from the church dangerously changed. God has said that no one can see Him and live (Ex. 33:20). If we really meet Christ, the false part of ourselves will *not* live. We find this scary, and some part of us shrinks from it.

When we rise from our beds, therefore, we must consciously determine to meet Christ, who waits for us in the Liturgy, even if this encounter will hurt and change us. For it will only hurt our false selves; the pain that we endure brings our ultimate healing. So, when we open our eyes on Sunday morning, we must act and speak as those who will soon meet Christ. This affects how we relate to one another on the way to church. How can we speak cruel and cutting things to our family members on the way to the service and then expect Christ to bless us at the chalice? How can we open our mouths to insult others just hours or minutes before opening our mouths to receive Christ's Body and Blood? We take our first steps in the "Communion line" when we step from our beds. We must arise in expectation and walk in humility and kindness as we journey to the Kingdom.

Chapter 2

"Blessed Is the Kingdom!"

The Liturgy we pray today has undergone many changes, developments, and evolutions in the past centuries. It begins now with the mighty and triumphal opening benediction, "Blessed is the Kingdom of the Father and of the Son and of the Holy Spirit!" to which the assembled Church responds, "Amen!" (The Church added this opening exclamation in about the eleventh century.) As the celebrant chants this, he takes the Holy Gospel in his hands and blesses the altar table with it, making the sign of the cross over the place where the sacrament of the Kingdom is to be celebrated, thus preparing the table for its holy use.

Significantly, our eucharistic worship opens with this glorious exclamation of joy, blessing the name of the Triune God for the Kingdom and salvation that He gives us. Through this opening cry we utter a prophetic shout of defiance; we throw down a gauntlet before the feet of the world, offering a ringing challenge to all the dying and deadly values of this age. For the world around us, the earthly land in which we celebrate that Liturgy, is a world of lies. In all our media—the magazines and books we read, the newscasts we watch, the movies we enjoy, the ads that flood our daily grind—the world ceaselessly calls us to bless false gods: the idols of Mammon, Success, Health, Youth, Beauty (as defined by the latest airbrushed models), Fame. From cradle to grave, falsehood bombards us.

Bless Mammon! the world tells us—the financial bottom line is all that matters, so measure your worth by the size of your salaries and your stock portfolios. Money is the means to the good life, which everyone knows consists of good food, good wine, unceasing entertainment, and expensive holidays. Play the lottery. Buy life insurance and extended warranties. Buy low and sell high. Work all you can—even on Sundays. The more of these you cram into your lives, the more contented you will be.

Bless Youth and Beauty! Spend more money on concealing your true age than you spend on the poor. Use skin creams to smooth wrinkles, hair dyes to eliminate your grey hair, Botox injections to keep a youthful face. First of all you must divinize and absolutize a certain image (often of an underaged anorexic, always of someone young), and then strive with all your might to approximate this image yourself—or at least inwardly blame yourself if you cannot. Thus our culture offers all kinds of cosmetic surgeries, breast implants, liposuction, fad diets, diet clubs and support groups, tanning salons, electrolysis. Pursuit of inner beauty is utterly lost in the scramble to conform to the most recently canonized image of an outer beauty which, despite all our efforts, will one day pass away.

In all these cultural distortions, the Church recognizes her rivals, denouncing them as false gods that cannot save. The idolatrous quests for Mammon, Youth, or skin-deep Beauty can ultimately never satisfy the human heart. Our society calls upon us to bless these impotent deities and to affirm them as the ultimate realities. The Church, in the opening words of her Divine Liturgy, offers the only true alternative: instead of these idols, we will bless only the true God, Triune and undivided, the Father, the Son, and the Holy Spirit; and among all the alternative paths offered us in the world, we will bless and choose only His Kingdom as the true destination for the human race. And so in the opening benediction we make our cry of defiance. In it, we refuse all other paths and lift up the name of the Trinity alone. And when the celebrant proclaims this truth and this Kingdom, the assembled Church, destined for that Kingdom, responds, "Amen!"

In responding with the amen, we do not merely accept the celebrant's proclamation as true and align ourselves with God and His Kingdom against the false gods of the world. More than that, we also seal what has been said. The celebrant's benediction and prayer, through the amen, now becomes the prayer *of the Church*.

The amen is not superfluous, but essential, revealing the nature and dignity of the lay people in the Church. The celebrant cannot utter the amen to his own prayer, for that is the job of the assembled faithful; without them and their liturgical response, there can be no Liturgy and no Church. This is why the canons do not permit the priest to celebrate the Liturgy without a congregation. The Body of Christ consists of both priest and people and contains a multitude of callings, tasks, and offices. God calls some to serve as deacons. Others He calls to read, some to assist at the altar, some to sing or chant. Others are called to prepare the temple before the Liturgy even begins, still others to offer the liturgical responses led by the choir or cantor. (Like a body whose parts have a multitude of different functions, the Body of the Church has a multitude of functions, and each function is important.) But God calls *all* to function as part of the royal priesthood (see 1 Peter 2:9) and, with the celebrant, to offer the eucharistic sacrifice of praise. Giving the amen reveals the laity as the priest's concelebrants.

Without the liturgical amen of the people, the priest's opening benediction remains no more than his individual pious wish, his devout and private prayer. But when the congregation responds, "Amen," the priest's utterance becomes the opening prayer of the Church, the first note in the Church's song, the first movement of the journey to the Kingdom. The clergy are priests for no other reason than because they express the prayer of the royal priesthood, the Church. The bishop ordains the priest as a presbyter, an elder (Greek *presbuteros*), his official title. The Church also refers to the presbyter as a priest (Greek *iereus*) because he embodies the priesthood of the Church—which in turn embodies the eternal priesthood of Christ, the only true Priest. By uttering this first amen, the laity reveal themselves in all their divine dignity as the priestly people of God.

Chapter 3

The Great Litany

Having declared our defiance of the world in the opening benediction, we now take our first step together in the journey, the great litany. We call it the "great" litany not just because of its length, but also because it sums up the totality of our needs. The Church here sweeps up the whole world in its great and loving arms, and offers it up to God to be blessed and sanctified and saved. The job of a priest is to offer sacrifice, and the Church, as God's royal priesthood, offers the world back to God.

In this intercessory offering, the Church leaves out no aspect of human existence. The Church surveys all the earth with its swarming, teeming activity and toil and offers it up to the Lord.

"In peace let us pray to the Lord." The Church begins by inviting all to pray "in peace," invoking first of all "the peace from above" and "the salvation of our souls." Because of this, some call this litany "the peace litany." Peace is fundamental not only to this prayer, but to all prayer and to the Christian life itself. Without internal peace, we cannot know God, much less come before Him as His priesthood and offer acceptable intercession. (For this reason the faithful exchange "the peace" later in the service before the prayer of the Eucharist, the **anaphora**, is offered.)

Peace is the great and parting gift of Christ to His Church. On His final night with the apostles, the Lord said, "Peace I leave with you, My peace I give to you; not as the world gives do I give to you" (John 14:27). Before Christ, warfare raged in the cosmos and in our hearts as well. By His saving death on the Cross and by the shedding of His precious blood, Christ brought peace to all (Col. 1:19–20). By repentance and faith, we enter into this saving peace. We have peace with God, with

> **Anaphora** (literally "offering")— The long prayer which, said by the priest over the gifts of bread and wine, by God's power transforms them into the Body and Blood of Christ

whom we are now reconciled (Rom. 5:1), and peace with each other as well. Indeed, the more we enter into this peace, the closer we draw to God and the more powerfully He dwells within us. That is why St. Seraphim of Sarov said, "Acquire the Spirit of peace, and thousands will be saved around you." So before we begin this litany, we are called to enter again into the peace of Christ, casting out from our hearts all distractions, all turmoil and anxiety, and focusing only on Christ. Only then can we stand aright before Him and offer supplication for the needs of all.

Having taken her stand in Christ's peace, the Church then prays for "the peace of the whole world." In this petition, the Church beseeches God to "break the bow and cut the spear in two and burn the chariot in the fire," "scattering the peoples *who* delight in war" (Ps. 46:9; 68:30). The Church thus supports and undergirds the efforts of all who work for peace in our war-torn world—soldiers, diplomats, aid workers. Those who serve in this challenging and difficult task (made more difficult in days vexed by constant threat of terrorism) may be tempted to discouragement and despair. They may think their work hopeless and beyond their strength. But in this petition, the Church invokes a strength beyond theirs; and all such workers for peace, whether Christian or not, are helped by the Christian God, the Savior and Lover of all men, and the Giver of peace to His world.

In this litany, the Church also prays for the head of the civil government "and for all civil authorities, and for the armed forces." That is, she prays for peace at home also, that all those who govern may do so justly and wisely, and that the nation in which the local church finds herself may know tranquility. This indeed is exactly what St. Paul commanded the Church to pray for whenever her members assembled: "I exhort first of all that supplications, prayers, intercessions, *and* giving of thanks be made for all men, for kings and all who are in authority, that we may lead a quiet and peaceable life in all godliness and reverence" (1 Tim. 2:1–2). Surveying the political landscape may tempt one at times to give up on politicians and on the political process in general, to say that all politicians are crooks and that voting and civil duty are useless. The Church, in this petition, disagrees. Whatever the weaknesses of politicians and the political process, the proper response is not cynicism and withdrawal, but prayer. For in whatever political system we find ourselves—be it American democracy or Byzantine autocracy or even totalitarian dictatorship—God can use the ruling powers to fulfill His purposes. In the first century, Paul commanded the Church to pray for the ruler of the Roman Empire, saying that God had ordained all these governing authorities (1 Tim. 2:1f; Rom. 13:1ff)—and the ruler at that time was the infamous Nero! How much more should we, in our day in the democratic West, pray for our rulers?

In this litany, the Church also prays for "the stability of the holy churches of God and for the unity of all." It prays for "this holy house and for those who enter with faith, reverence, and the fear of God." It prays for its local bishop by name, "for the honorable priesthood, the diaconate in Christ, for all the clergy and the people." In this petition, we see the saving synergy (or cooperation) in action. Of course we must do all we can to help the Church fulfill its mission: we must work for unity among all Orthodox and strive to resolve whatever quarrels threaten to separate us. By patience and goodwill, we must work to make our parishes places of love and mutual support. We must support our clergy, bishops, priests, deacons, and all who do the work of the Church, giving them due honor and supplying their material needs. But for all our efforts, the health of the Church ultimately does not lie with us. It lies with God. That is why we pray for the Church in these petitions, for all our toil will be fruitless if God does not bless it.

The Church also prays for the physical world on which we all depend. We pray for "seasonable weather, for abundance of the fruits of the earth, and for peaceful times" to harvest these gifts. Long before it became fashionable to be "green," long before journalists spoke about ecology and the environment, long before people began debating about the Kyoto Accord, the Church knew of the importance of soil and weather, of earth and sky. Food does not come from the supermarket, whatever city-dwellers might imagine. It comes from the earth, and its harvest and supply depend on seasonable weather, on rain and sunshine, on freedom from drought and blight and war. Thus our food and welfare come ultimately from God. The Church does not forget this, even though she has always been anchored in the cities and has thrived in them (see the petition about "every city and countryside," which shows that the cities were the main centers of the churches). And so the Church, as God's priesthood for the whole world, lifts this up to God.

In the great litany, the Church also prays for those in special distress and danger: for "travelers by land, by sea, and by air" (in ancient times especially, travel was dangerous), for "the sick and the suffering," for "captives and their deliverance." Indeed, the Church prays for our deliverance from "all affliction, wrath, danger, and need." In earth's dark and dangerous places, many people think themselves alone and abandoned—the elderly sick woman lying in pain in her small apartment without medical insurance; the Western journalist held captive by terrorists; the young child abused by a family member, frightened and with no one to turn to. But God has not abandoned any of these. The Church is the friend of the world, and it commends all those in need to God, who has revealed Himself as the hope of the hopeless, the protector of widows and the father of orphans. No tear falls that our God does not see, no fear grips the human heart that leaves our God untouched, and the Church intercedes for all those in distress.

To each of these petitions and needs, the faithful lift up the cry, "Lord, have mercy!" (Greek *Kyrie eleison*). Though the English word "mercy" has a rather juridical feel (recalling the plea of a condemned man for mercy and pardon from a judge), the Greek has a wider meaning. In this repeated response, the Church prays not only for pardon, but for blessing, strength, rescue, the total outpouring of God's generosity. The "mercy" we beg is the equivalent of the Hebrew term *hesed*, variously translated not only "mercy" (in the King James Version), but also "steadfast love," "lovingkindness." In this litany we cry for God's covenant loyalty, His faithfulness revealed to His children in acts of saving strength. When we pray over and over again, "Lord, have mercy!" we are beseeching the God of our fathers to lift us up from all the pits into which we stumble.

At the culmination of all these petitions, we "commemorate our most holy, most pure, most blessed and glorious Lady Theotokos and ever-virgin Mary, with all the saints." A Christian in this world never stands before the Lord alone, but always as part of the vast family of God, the Church of Christ. As a family, we rely on the prayers of the rest of the Church—especially the prayers of the holy Theotokos, the first Christian, the one who leads us in the heavenly praises of the Trinity. Our blessed Lady loves us for the sake of her Son, and in her loving intercession we take refuge. In the company of this heavenly throng we "commend ourselves and each other and all our life to Christ our God," expecting from Him alone the salvation of our souls and the answers to our prayers.

The prayer that currently follows this litany not only asks by a general petition that God would "look down upon us and this holy house with pity" and hear our prayers. Like all prayers, it also sets forth the Church's theology. The God to whom we pray transcends by far all our puny and inadequate understandings of Him. This prayer describes Him in a series of four negative adjectives: "incomparable, incomprehensible, immeasurable, inexpressible." This is true apophatic theology: God cannot be adequately described; He can only be experienced in wonder. No words can do Him justice, for the God with whom we have to do defies all limitations. We can only stand mute, lost in adoration before God's power, glory, mercy, and love for mankind. We rightly trumpet the greatness of God in this prayer, for only a God this great could cradle the world with all its needs, caring for each one.

Unbelievers have long poured scorn on the Church's faith, saying how presumptuous and audacious the Christians are to assert that their little prayers could change the vast universe and its affairs. The unbelievers are correct: our faith is audacious—and true. Having known Him who toppled death from his dark throne and who has "bestowed resurrection on the fallen" (from the **kontakion** of Pascha), we are indeed audacious and bold enough to declare that our God, great enough to hold together the whole universe, still condescends to hear and answer our prayers. He who loved us enough to die and overthrow death also loves us enough to hear us when we call to Him over lesser things.

> **Kontakion (or kondak)—** A brief liturgical hymn that gives the meaning of a feast day; often paired with *troparion* (or tropar)

One final historical note: The great litany originally did not come at this point in the service. Rather, it formed the intercessory prayers of the people after the reading of the lessons and the dismissal of the catechumens. During the ninth century, it came to be offered also right after the so-called "little entrance" with the Gospel book, before the **trisagion**, and was sometimes called the "litany of the trisagion." Around the eleventh century, the Church began to recite it in its present position as well, immediately before the antiphons. Only from the thirteenth century onwards was it recited at its present place and there only. What is the significance of these developments?

> **Trisagion—** (literally "thrice-holy," from the Greek *tri*, three, and *agios*, holy)— The hymn or prayer "Holy God, Holy Mighty, Holy Immortal, have mercy on us."

I would suggest that this change in position reveals the pastoral heart of the Church. In the present form of the Byzantine Liturgy, the first thing the faithful do when they assemble is to pray for the world. It is as if the Church feels an urgency about the world's needs and cannot wait to run to meet those needs. Before the assembly does anything else—before the initial praises of the antiphons, before the celebrant and people formally greet and bless one another, before the reading of the Holy Scriptures—the Church kneels before the needy of the earth in an intercessory act of *kenosis* (self-emptying) to pray for the whole world. Christ is the Savior of the world and, following her divine Lord, the Church also keeps the whole world close to her heart.

Chapter 4

The Antiphons

After praying the great litany, the assembly takes three more steps towards its Kingdom destination by singing the three **antiphons.**

These antiphons have a fascinating history. Unlike today, when each parish in a city functions separately as a self-contained unit, in the days of St. John Chrysostom in the fourth century, in cities like Constantinople all the Orthodox churches in the city formed a single integrated whole. The main church in the city served the Liturgy on Sundays, and all the people of the city went to that Liturgy. The people of the city all belonged to the main church, but also went together to the other churches when called to do so, such as on feast days. (In the cities of those days, small by comparison with modern cities, such processions were possible.) On the feast day of St. John the Forerunner, for example, the people would form a procession to go from the main church to the church of St. John to serve the Liturgy there, and they would sing hymns as they went. These hymns were the antiphons. In the days of St. John Chrysostom, the cantor would chant a verse or two of the psalm, and the people would sing the refrain; the cantor would chant the next few verses of the psalm, and the people would sing the refrain again, and so on. The people came to like these hymns so much that they eventually became a fixed part of the Liturgy, even when there was no procession on the way to church.

The antiphons sung in church in the eighth century included Psalm 92 (with the refrain "Through the prayers of the Theotokos, O Savior, save us!"), Psalm 93 (with the refrain "Alleluia!") and Psalm 95 (with the hymn "Only-begotten Son," written by the Emperor Justinian in the sixth century, as its refrain). (Psalm 94 was passed

> **Antiphon—** A hymn originally sung antiphonally, that is, with alternating voices or choirs; now used to designate the three opening hymns of the Liturgy

over because parts of it were thought a bit too bloodthirsty, with its references to "O LORD God, to whom vengeance belongs . . . cut them off in their own wickedness.")

Everything that is alive grows and develops, and this includes living liturgical tradition. Thus the way the Church sang the antiphons continued to develop too. In the twelfth century some monks in Constantinople began the (then) innovative custom of substituting Psalms 103 and 146 and the Beatitudes for the normal antiphons at the Sunday Liturgy. Today some churches (such as those in the Russian tradition) follow this custom, while other churches (those in the Greek tradition) follow the original custom of singing Psalms 92, 93, and 95 as antiphons. Whichever hymns are used, all liturgies today begin with the singing of three antiphons.

The exuberant praise of God that forms our early liturgical steps into the Kingdom is no accident, for our spiritual life consists of praise. Christ recreated us for this very purpose, to "proclaim the praises of Him who called you out of darkness into His marvelous light" (1 Peter 2:9). Praising God is not simply *one* thing we do; it is *everything*. All that we do must be an act of praise, for God calls us to offer ourselves to Him as a doxology of living flesh and blood. The psalmist sings, "Let every breath praise the Lord" (Ps. 150:6 LXX), and as disciples of Christ we strive to fulfill this, making every breath, every word, every action, every thought and intention an offering of praise to our God.

The world has grown dark and silent because it remains unillumined by the praise of God. C. S. Lewis, in his science fiction trilogy, coined the word "Thulcandra" as the angels' name for the planet Earth. The "thulc-" part of the title, Lewis said, is a combination of the words "thick" and "sulk." It is meant to convey sadness, moroseness, petulance. The planet Earth, in Lewis's trilogy, has become "the silent planet," one that has turned its back on God and refuses to join in the cosmic song of God's praise chanted by the angels. Our race alone sits in sulky silence, out of step with all the rest of the vast, teeming universe. All the rest of creation—the angels, archangels, dominions, thrones, powers, cherubim, seraphim—all of God's innumerable and varied hosts unite in one joyous chorus, all lift up a jubilant song, standing on exultant tiptoe (as it were), and turning their shining faces to the King as they radiantly sing to Him their eternal hymns. At the beginning of the world's creation, all the angelic sons of God shouted for joy before Him (Job 38:7), and at the world's ending, all the angels will again pour out a chorus, a deafening roar like a cataract or booming thunder

(Rev. 19:6). Even now, all heaven and earth echo with the shout of praise:

> Then I looked, and I heard the voice of many angels around the throne, the living creatures, and the elders; and the number of them was ten thousand times ten thousand, and thousands of thousands, saying with a loud voice:
>
> > "Worthy is the Lamb who was slain
> > To receive power and riches and wisdom,
> > And strength and honor and glory and blessing!"
>
> And every creature which is in heaven and on the earth and under the earth and such as are in the sea, and all that are in them, I heard saying:
>
> > "Blessing and honor and glory and power
> > Be to Him who sits on the throne,
> > And to the Lamb, forever and ever!" (Rev. 5:11–13)

All of creation extols its God with full-throated praise. The human race alone sits in darkness and isolation like spoiled children, refusing joy, refusing light, refusing to play at the Father's feet. We alone refuse to join in the universal song.

God meant Man to lead the creation in its praise of Him. Sin has deprived us of our place at the head of the chorus; it has driven us out and sealed the lips created to praise our Maker. Christ, the Lamb whose death takes away the sin of the world, ends this fatal isolation and opens our lips that our mouth may show forth God's praise (Ps. 51:15, verses said by the priest before serving the Liturgy). In Christ we return to join the rest of creation, taking our rightful place as leaders in the choir. The Liturgy begins with this antiphonal praise because our salvation consists of praise.

Between the antiphons of praise, the priest offers prayers. Originally, when the people sang the antiphons in procession on the way to church, the deacon introduced each prayer by saying, "Let us pray to the Lord!" after which the priest said a prayer and the people responded by saying, "Amen." Later, the priests said their prayers silently, and the deacon expanded his diaconal invitation to pray by chanting other petitions as well to give the priest time to say his prayer quietly, apart from the people. Thus the "little litany" was born, with the deacon chanting the petitions, "Again and again in peace, let us pray to the Lord," then, "Help us, save us, have mercy on us and keep us, O God, by Your grace," and then finally, "Commemorating our most holy, most pure, most blessed Lady the Theotokos and ever-virgin Mary, with all the saints." After the deacon finished this little litany, the priest would chant aloud the final exclamation of his prayer so that the people could respond with the amen.

The prayers offered after the first and second antiphons are not simply "filler," but cries to God from His children, asking Him to preserve us and accept us as we draw near to Him. We ask Him to save us and bless us, since we come to Him as His own inheritance. We ask Him to preserve the fullness of His Church by filling us with Himself and His glory; we ask Him to sanctify us, since we love the beauty of His house and come there to worship Him, and to abide with us forever, since we put our hope in Him. Speaking to Christ, who promised that when two or three would gather in His name (Matt. 18:20), He would be there to answer their requests, we boldly offer our petitions. These prayers reveal why we dare to draw near to God and dare to walk in procession right into His holy presence: we are no mere collection of ordinary persons, but the Church of the living God, His inheritance, His joy, His covenant people. We have come to Him because He has called us.

Finally, during the third antiphon, the clergy and their attendants make a procession with the Gospel. This is a vestige of the original practice of the clergy entering the church for the first time at the beginning of the Liturgy, bringing the Gospel book with them. In the days of St. John Chrysostom, the clergy would enter the church with the Gospel book and go straight into the altar, so that the service proper could begin. The Gospel book was carried for a practical purpose only—the deacon (who kept the Gospel book in his home for safekeeping) brought it with him to church so that he could read it during the service. But now that the Church keeps the Gospel book on the altar table, the carrying of it in procession has a deeper meaning: it shows that Christ is among us, and we venerate the Gospel book as we would Christ, carrying it reverently, with joy, in high triumph, with an honor guard of lights and incense. In some traditions, the faithful press forward to kiss the Gospel book as it passes by, offering their love to Christ, whose saving words the book contains. We do not sing the antiphons and all the Divine Liturgy in memory of one who is dead and parted from us. We sing as an explosion of joy at finding Christ alive and in our midst. The Gospel procession during the third antiphon reveals what our thunderous singing is all about.

Chapter 5

The Entrance
and the Trisagion

After the antiphons, we take the next step in our journey, the entrance with the Gospel, sometimes called "the little entrance" to distinguish it from "the great entrance" done later with the gifts of bread and wine. Today the entrance is made in the following way: the clergy leave the altar area through one of the deacon's (or side) doors and proceed into the main body of the Church (the **nave**) carrying the Gospel book. After the third antiphon is completed, the deacon cries, "Wisdom! Stand upright!" and the clergy reenter the altar area through the royal (or central) doors.

> **Nave**
> (literally, "ship")—
> The main
> body of the
> church
> building,
> where the
> faithful gather
> for the
> services

The meaning of this entrance appeared more readily in the days of St. John Chrysostom, when it actually was the initial entrance of all the clergy and faithful into the church building. In those days, the celebrant would come before the main outer doors of the church and pray the prayer of the entrance. Then he and his fellow clergy would enter the church and proceed straight into the altar as all the faithful entered the nave. In today's Liturgy, the entrance is not so much an *entrance* as it is a *circuit*—the priest does not simply *enter* the altar area, but rather *exits* the altar and makes a circular procession through the nave, returning again to the altar from which he began.

But however the entrance is done, its meaning remains the same: the Church solemnly enters into God's holy presence, becoming the liturgical assembly of the people of God. Though scattered through the world, living separately in their individual homes, the faithful together form one single family. Every Sunday the individual Christians who make up a parish leave their homes and journey to the church temple. Having left the world and exited this fallen and dying age, they then assemble in one place, entering the church and God's eternal Kingdom. This spiritual entry is given expression as the little entrance. It is not just the clergy entering the altar. It is the entry of the whole Church into the presence of God.

Such an act of boldness calls for bravery. Who are we, children of dust and ashes, sinners who drink iniquity like water (Job 15:16), to stand before the thrice-holy God and offer our puny songs? How can we find the courage to sing our songs to Him who is hymned by countless myriads of angels? To find this boldness, just before the entrance the celebrant prays the prayer of the entrance: "O Master, Lord our God, who appointed in heaven orders and hosts of angels and archangels for the service of Your glory: grant that with our entrance there may be an entrance of holy angels, serving with us and glorifying Your goodness."

In the Divine Liturgy, we are not alone in our praises. As the prophet Elisha once told his servant, "Those who *are* with us *are* more than those who *are* with them" (2 Kings 6:16)—the invisible angels worshipping with us vastly outnumber the worshippers we see with our eyes. Though there may be only a few people in church, the building is still thronged with multitudes of the heavenly hosts. In the Divine Liturgy we join our voices (however little and trembling they may be) to a mighty heavenly chorus. The orders and hosts of angels and archangels stand about God's throne and chant their thrice-holy hymn. God calls us, in Christ, to serve with them and join them in glorifying His goodness through our songs. Here is encouragement to sing! Listening to the music we make (in some cases perhaps not very tunefully), we may be tempted to discouragement. But God listens with keener ears than ours and hears the music ascending from our hearts as well. If the music we make is not all that we would like (humanly speaking), it is drowned out in the thunderous song of the angels, whose chorus we join.

This prayer of the entrance reveals something else fundamental to our worship: its location. Our worship does not take place on earth, but in heaven, for the angels enter with us and serve with us as we together glorify God. Where do the angels stand as they sing to God? Not on earth—before His throne in heaven. Therefore our worship actually takes place in heaven, before God's very throne, for in the Liturgy we ascend from earth to heaven. St. Paul teaches this too: God has made us sit with Christ in the heavenly places (Eph. 2:6). We are citizens of the Kingdom (Phil. 3:20), and in the Liturgy we return to our homeland, having access to the Father in heaven by the Spirit (Eph. 2:18). We may think the Divine Liturgy takes place in Vancouver or New York, in London or Moscow, but it does not. These are merely the cities in which the local churches gather. The Divine Liturgy occurs in the Kingdom, and the interior of the church temple is made resplendent with its icons and outward glory to reflect this heavenly reality.

As the third antiphon reaches its conclusion, the deacon sings out, "Wisdom! Stand upright!" and the introit verse is sung: "Come, let us worship and fall down before Christ, who rose from the dead. O Son of God, save us who sing to You! Alleluia!" The deacon lifts high the Gospel book, making the sign of the cross with it to bless the entrance. The clergy and attendants then enter the altar.

There are only a few times in the Divine Liturgy when the deacon exhorts the faithful to "stand upright"—here at the little entrance; just before the Gospel is read; and again at the beginning of the anaphora, when he tells them to "stand aright." If any in the congregation are sitting, slouching, or leaning, they are exhorted to straighten up and stand erect. Our entrance into the presence of Christ is about to culminate, and we must stand straight to greet our King.

Some might think that posture does not matter, and that as long as a person pays attention in the heart, the bodily position is irrelevant. If we were angels, that might be so. Presumably the holy bodiless powers (as they are called) do not have to worry about physical posture, but man is not bodiless. It is not so much the case that we *have* bodies; rather, we *are* bodies. Since we are a compound of spirit and matter, what our bodies do also affects our spirits. That is why the church bids us make prostrations during Great Lent, for the humbling of the body helps to humble the spirit. In the same way, standing up straight and tall helps us attend to the presence of Christ in our midst. By standing upright, "at attention," we heighten our attitude of expectancy as we enter the presence of God.

As the clergy and their attendants enter the altar through the royal doors and take their places, the people sing the **troparia**, or hymns of the day. Originally these hymns were refrains of the third antiphon, and on great feasts of the Lord they still serve as such antiphonal refrains. The number of appointed troparia has multiplied through the years and now they have taken on a life of their own, separated from the antiphons to which they were once attached. Now they declare the themes of the Liturgy of the day, including hymns about the

> **Troparion** (plural **troparia**)— a brief liturgical hymn commemorating a feast day, often paired with a *kontakion*

Resurrection (on Sunday), about the saint of the day or the special feast being celebrated, and about the saint to whom the temple is dedicated. As we sing them or listen to them sung, we can hear the Church teaching us her liturgical theology, transmitting to us the meaning and content of our faith. For these are not simply poetic or pretty choruses, but the dogmas of the Church set to music. In listening intently to the troparia, we learn what the Church teaches about the Lord, the Mother of God, the saints, and the great saving events of the faith. The time for the singing of the troparia is thus not a time to let the mind wander or to wait passively for the next thing to happen. It is a time to open ears and heart and drink deeply from the living waters of the Church's dogmas.

As the final part of the entrance, after the clergy have entered the altar, we sing the trisagion hymn. In Constantinople in the early sixth century, the people sang the trisagion as the entry chant. The cantor would sing verses of Psalm 80 with the repeated refrain, "Holy God, Holy Mighty, Holy Immortal, have mercy on us!" during which the clergy entered the church and went into the altar. (We see vestiges of this psalm during the trisagion when a bishop serves.) In the years following the sixth century, as the service developed, the psalm dropped away, leaving only the refrain, "Holy God, Holy Mighty, Holy Immortal, have mercy on us!" repeated three times, followed by the "Glory to the Father and to the Son and to the Holy Spirit, now and ever and unto ages of ages. Amen" which originally formed the conclusion of the psalm. In our present practice, the original function of the trisagion as an entry chant has been obscured. The trisagion hymn, however, still serves as the culmination of the entry into the altar.

Thus, it still takes some daring to sing this hymn. For this is the hymn of the angels who stand before the Lord of glory with covered faces. The trisagion hymn is an expansion of the thrice-holy hymn found in Isaiah's vision. In chapter six of his prophecy, Isaiah relates a vision he had of the God of Israel: God sat on His throne, high and lifted up, the hem of His robe filling the temple. The six-winged seraphim stood above Him in all their fiery brilliance (the Hebrew word *seraphim* means "fiery ones"); with two wings they covered their faces, with two they covered their feet, and with two they flew. And always they called out in wonder to one another, "Holy, holy, holy, Lord of Hosts! The whole earth is full of Your glory!" The Orthodox hymnographer took this passage as the basis for the trisagion hymn, expanding the angelic "holy, holy, holy" into "Holy God, Holy Mighty, Holy Immortal."

To stand before the heavenly God takes daring, and therefore the clergy offer a prayer before joining the faithful in singing this hymn. Often the clergy pray this prayer silently during the singing of the troparia. But it is the prayer of the people, and the people say amen to it immediately before singing the trisagion. Should they not then hear the prayer to which they say amen?

The prayer of the trisagion is a theological masterpiece, balancing God's transcendent holiness and His saving condescension. It begins by invoking the "holy God" who "rests among the holy ones," the angelic hosts in heaven, the One who is "hymned by the seraphim with the thrice-holy cry and glorified by the cherubim, and worshipped by every heavenly power." This is the God we sinners dare to approach, this the mighty chorus we dare to join. But we are not dismayed before such holiness, nor do we shrink back from Him, for He has revealed His great condescension to us: "out of nothing He brought all things into being" as a sheer act of unconstrained love; He "created man after His own image and likeness, adorning him with His every gift, giving him wisdom and understanding." In creation He lavishes His love upon us, and even when we fell away He did not turn against us. He "does not despise the sinner, but instead has appointed repentance unto salvation," always looking for our return, like the father looking for the return of his prodigal son. And despite our countless acts of infidelity to His love, "even in this hour," after we have sinned against Him so many times, "He has granted us to stand before the glory of His holy altar and to offer the worship and praise which are His due." Weak and sinful though we are, He calls us to approach Him.

Because of such innumerable blessings poured out upon us, we now boldly ask Him to "accept even from the mouths of us sinners the thrice-holy hymn" which the angels in heaven offer Him. In return for our puny praises, we ask Him to "forgive us every transgression, sanctify our souls and bodies, and enable us to serve Him in holiness all the days of our life." That is, we ask Him to bless us even more, pardoning our sins and transforming our weakness into strength. In this prayer, we do not stand before God alone, but as part of a great heavenly company, stretching back through history to the very beginning; we offer our prayer "through the intercessions of the holy Theotokos and of all the saints who from the beginning of the world have been well-pleasing to You." Only after offering this intercession does the Church lift up her voice to hymn her King with the words of the angels, standing before the very throne of the heavenly Lord.

Chapter 6

The First Blessing

During the singing of the trisagion hymn, the clergy leave their places at the altar table and proceed to the **high place.** The high place is, as its name suggests, an elevated place at the extreme east end of the church temple in which, classically, are a number of seats. The central throne, often a little more luxurious than the others beside it, is reserved for the bishop, with the other thrones for the priests who concelebrate with him. Even if the bishop is not present at the Liturgy, the presiding priest never sits in the bishop's seat (or "cathedra"), but keeps it reserved for him alone, as a mark of respect. (In some churches, this seat is placed elsewhere, in the nave of the church.)

> **High Place—**
> The place at the far east end of the altar area where the bishop's chair was located

As this brief procession approaches the thrones, the deacon asks the main celebrant to bless them, saying, "Bless, master, the high place." The celebrant responds by invoking the name of God and blessing the high place with the sign of the cross, saying, "Blessed are You on the throne of Your glorious Kingdom, who sit upon the cherubim, always, now and ever and unto ages of ages." Before sitting upon their own clerical thrones, the clergy bless God who sits on His throne in heaven, acknowledging that all authority comes from Him.

This procession is a survival from the time of St. John Chrysostom in the fourth century. In those days, the service began when the bishop entered the altar area, blessed the thrones on which he and his clergy were to sit, greeted the assembled faithful with a greeting of peace, and then sat down for the readings of Scripture. Though now other things (such as the singing of the antiphons) precede this original beginning, the clergy still go in procession to their seats for the Scripture readings as they did in the days of St. John Chrysostom. Things change very slowly in the Orthodox Church!

When the celebrant reaches the high place, he then turns to greet the people. (This is the practice of those following the Slavic liturgical traditions. For those following the Greek liturgical tradition, this greeting has been lost.) In the days of St. John Chrysostom, the people could make a great hubbub and noise when they came to church, and so the deacon first had to ask them to quiet down. That is what the deacon's cry to the people, "Let us attend!" originally meant—stop talking and listen up! Even now, when hopefully the faithful are already quiet and attentive in church, the deacon's cry directs our focus to the altar and heightens our sense of anticipation.

The celebrant then greets the people, blessing them with the sign of the cross from the high place, saying, "Peace be unto all!" The faithful respond to his greeting by greeting him in return, saying, "And to your spirit!" (Nowadays, this response is sometimes given in the name of the people by the reader alone.)

In places where this blessing is given, it is easy to miss the significance of this brief exchange and to regard it as some meaningless religious formality introducing the readings. But this blessing of the people and the response that follows it are important, for they reveal essential characteristics of the Liturgy. Firstly, the celebrant does not simply greet the people, acknowledging their presence, but in the Byzantine liturgical traditions, he invokes God's peace upon them. Such greetings have a long history in the Bible. *"Shalom!"* ("Peace!") was the usual Jewish greeting (compare our Lord's greeting to the disciples after His Resurrection in John 20:19: "Peace *be* with you"). But its use by Christians meant something more than the usual mere formality. The greeting was not simply a *wish* for peace—it was also a *bestowal* of it. When the Lord, for example, sent the Twelve out on their first mission, He told them whenever they entered a village to find the house of someone worthy and respectable and greet them. "If the household is worthy," He said, "let your peace come upon it. But if it is not worthy, let your peace return to you" (Matt. 10:11–13).

In the Liturgy, the celebrant is therefore not simply greeting the people in a kind of religious version of "Hi there." He is bestowing the peace of God upon his fellow-members of Christ's Body. Christ Himself is our peace (Eph. 2:14), and His presence rests upon His people as they assemble. By invoking peace upon them, the celebrant bestows the presence of the Lord Himself. In the Divine Liturgy, Christ is truly in our midst, and this presence transforms us. In the world, we know only turmoil, fear, and anxiety. "In the world," Christ said, "you will have tribulation" (John 16:33). But in the Liturgy we have left the world, and worldly fears can no longer eat away at us, for Christ, the peace that passes all understanding (Phil. 4:7), calms all our anxieties and keeps our hearts. This priestly bestowal of peace reveals the Liturgy as the presence of Christ, before whose face all fears fade away.

The timing of this blessing is important, for, having assembled, we receive the Lord's peace as the preparation for hearing His Word. We cannot absorb the Word of God with distracted hearts. If our minds are in a turmoil, we cannot hear what God is saying, for anxiety has a way of filling the human heart and leaving no space there for anything else. We must first cast out all anxiety to make a space within us to receive God's Word. Only when we are at peace, settled in before God and at rest in Him, can we attend inwardly to what He has to say to us.

The first blessing reveals something else fundamental about the Divine Liturgy: its dialogic nature. There are other dialogues between the clergy and the people in the Liturgy:

- The priest speaks to the people and blesses them just before the reading of the Gospel.
- At the peace, the priest bestows his blessing upon the people, saying, "Peace be unto all!" and they return the blessing, saying, "And with your spirit!"
- The anaphora opens with an extended dialogue, as the priest says to the people, "The grace of the Lord Jesus Christ and the love of God and the communion of the Holy Spirit be with all of you!" and they respond to him, "And with your spirit!" The priest then says, "Let us lift up our hearts!" to which they reply, "We lift them up to the Lord!" The priest continues, "Let us give thanks to the Lord!" while they reply, "It is meet and right to worship the Father and the Son and the Holy Spirit, the Trinity, one in essence and undivided!"
- After the anaphora the priest blesses the faithful, saying, "May the mercies of our great God and Savior Jesus Christ be with all of you!" and they reply, "And with your spirit!"
- After the Lord's Prayer, the priest again says, "Peace be unto all!" receiving the reply, "And to your spirit!"
- At the conclusion of the service, the priest bids the faithful depart, saying, "Let us depart in peace," while they reply, "In the name of the Lord!"

Given the fact that the Liturgy is primarily addressed to God, priest and people talk to each other a great deal! This dialogic characteristic of the Divine Liturgy reveals that the priest and people stand together in a unity of encouragement. The priest does not stand apart from the people, as if he were the source of blessing and they simply the passive recipients of his blessing. Rather, they both stand together in a fundamental solidarity of need, both needing blessing from God, both needing encouragement. The priest indeed blesses the people and encourages them to draw near to God. But they also bless him in return, and encourage him to draw near to God with them. Though priest and layman may have different liturgical roles and duties, all alike stand in need of encouragement and of receiving blessing from their common Lord.

Chapter 7

The Readings, Gospel, & Homily

After the priestly blessing come the readings from the Holy Scriptures, which culminate with the reading of the Holy Gospel. In our modern days of mass-produced literature, when almost every day brings printed "junk mail" into our homes and when we are almost drowning in the written word, both on the printed page and online, it is easy to miss how important the readings were to the early Christians. To understand the significance of the readings, we need to escape from our word-congested modern age and travel back to the past.

The Christian Church, built as it was upon the foundation of Judaism, is a Bible Church, finding its joy in *ta biblia*, "the books." From the days of the apostles the Christians would meet together in a *synaxis* (or "gathering") for the purpose of listening to readings from the Scriptures, much as Jews in the time of Christ met together in a synagogue to listen to the Law of Moses and the words of the Prophets. People then were not saturated with and desensitized to the written word as they are today, and would eagerly gather to hear someone read from a book. We perhaps find it difficult today to imagine the anticipation and delight that accompanied these readings. The reader proclaimed wisdom gathered from the ages past, making carefully preserved saving illumination and truth available to all with ears to hear, and those who sought wisdom came running and stood openmouthed to receive it. The Christians of those early days would delight to have huge amounts of Scripture read to them. Not all people in those days of the early Church could afford to own books (since books had to be copied by hand, and therefore were very expensive), and for many Christians these *synaxes* formed their main exposure to the Scriptures.

The Church read so much Scripture in those early days that her faithful needed a break from listening! In between the readings, the Church inserted a psalm that the faithful would chant, so that they alternated concentrated listening with spirited singing. These psalms were sung in the following way: the reader would sing the psalm verse that was to be sung as the refrain (the so-called **prokeimenon**, meaning that which "lies before" the appointed psalm). The people would sing that prokeimenon refrain after him. Then he would chant some of the psalm. The people would chime in with the appointed refrain; then came some more of the psalm by the reader, then the refrain by the people again. The Church chose psalms to fit in with the theme of the liturgical day and sang each according to its own particular melody or "tone." The refrain for the psalm just before the reading of the final Gospel lesson was always "Alleluia! Alleluia! Alleluia!" since this pre-Gospel psalm was a cry of joy that the words of Jesus were about to be heard.

> **Prokeimenon** (or **prokeimen**) — A liturgical verse chanted by the reader and repeated by the people that introduces the epistle reading at Liturgy

What did the Church read to her members in those early days? Until the eighth century, the series began with an Old Testament reading from the Prophets. St. Justin the Philosopher (who was martyred AD 165) wrote a description of the Liturgy of his day in his *Apology*. In it, he wrote, "On the day called Sunday, all gather together in one place and the memoirs of the apostles or the writings of the prophets are read, as long as time permits" (*Apology*, ch. 67). His reference to "as long as time permits" allows us to conclude that the Church did not hurry through this time of reading, but read great amounts of Holy Scripture to her faithful.

For some this reference to reading from the Old Testament may be surprising. It is easy for us to think that the Old Testament is for the Jews and the New Testament for the Christians, but in fact the entire Bible belongs to the Christian Church. Indeed, when the apostles referred to "the Scriptures" (as in Rom. 1:2; 1 Cor. 15:3; 2 Tim. 3:16; 2 Pet. 1:20) they meant the *Old* Testament, and even today the Old Testament Scriptures remain part of the Church's literary foundation. The Orthodox Church reads sections from the Old Testament at Great Vespers on the eve of the Twelve Great Feasts, as well as at the **Presanctified Liturgy** and during Holy Week. The Church condemns as heretical the tendency of some to devalue the Old Testament: indeed, a fellow named Marcion in the second century rejected the Old Testament as sub-Christian and was excommunicated! From the days of the apostles, the Old Testament formed part of the Church's lectionary and was read every Sunday.

The Church in the days of St. Justin also read the writings of the apostles (sometimes several selections, not just a single reading from one of the epistles). This practice also dates from apostolic days. When St. Paul and the other apostles wrote their letters (or "epistles") to the churches, these letters were read as part of the eucharistic gatherings. When, for example, the church in Corinth received a letter from Paul, they not only read it, reread it, and treasured it, but also passed around copies to churches in other cities so that they could share in its spiritual wealth too. Eventually, as these letters were passed from church to church in the first and second centuries, they became the common property of all. The New Testament was being born. The Church naturally read the writings of the apostles after the Old Testament, for the Church was built upon the foundation of their teaching (Eph. 2:20; Rev. 21:14).

After readings from the Old Testament and the writings of the apostles, the Church read from the four Gospels. (Later in the second century, semi-Christian heresies on the Church's fringe produced their own gospels, such as the so-called "Gospel of Judas," based not so much on historical fact or preserved apostolic memory as on their desire to produce an exotic and different kind of Christianity. Instead of preserving the remembered words of Jesus, they made up their own ideas and put them into the mouths of Jesus and the apostles. The apostolic Church always knew about these weird gospels, but would have nothing to do with them. For the real Church, what mattered were the authentic words of Jesus.)

These readings from the Gospels came last, as the crown and culmination of all the other readings. Everything led to Jesus—His was the voice they longed to hear, His the presence they had come together to experience. In reading from the Gospels last, the Church was saving the best for the last, the good wine until the end (see John 2:10). She knew all Scripture as authoritative and life-giving, but the words of the Lord Jesus were in a class by themselves. The Lord whom

Presanctified Liturgy (or **Liturgy of the Presanctified Gifts**)— The evening service served in the weekdays of Great Lent and Holy Week at which the Body and Blood of Christ, sanctified at the Liturgy the previous Sunday (or "presanctified") and kept until the Presanctified Liturgy the following week, are brought in and consumed as Holy Communion

the Christians loved, to whom they prayed, for whom they lived and died, was speaking directly to them. The Church experienced the Holy Gospels not as the words of a revered but dead philosopher, one who had taught them but now was with them no longer, but as the words of the Lord who lived among them still.

In today's Orthodox Church, the Scriptures still have pride of place, and they dominate the first part of the service like a diamond set among a cluster of jewels. Since the eighth century, the Old Testament lesson has dropped away, so that we read it no longer at the Sunday Eucharist. And the psalm placed between the Old Testament lesson and the New Testament epistle has largely dropped away, leaving only a verse to be recited as the prokeimenon. (The psalm for which the alleluia was the refrain has also shrunk down to a verse or two.) But the Scriptures remain as the living voice of the apostolic Church, and her faithful still delight to be fed on the heavenly manna of God's Word.

This delight is seen in the way the Church reads the Scriptures. They are not read casually, by anyone who happens to offer at the time. Rather, someone is set apart for this honored task, (traditionally) tonsured by the bishop as a reader, and (often) clothed in a special vestment called an **exorasson**. The reader first gets a blessing from the celebrant to read, since he is keenly aware of how awesome is his task. He is about to chant the words of the life-giving Scriptures, concerning which the Lord said, "It is easier for heaven and earth to pass away than for one tittle of the law to fail" (Luke 16:17). He dares not begin such a work without first asking God's blessing and strength to lend his own humble voice to make God's truth known to mortals.

> **Exorasson**
> (or **riassa**)—
> A long flowing black robe with long sleeves worn by clergy over their inner black vestment (or cassock). In some traditions it is also worn by cantors/choir directors.

Then the reader takes his stand in the midst of the community, and the deacon cries out, "Wisdom!"—first before the prokeimenon and then before the epistle. We should not overlook the significance of this brief exclamation. It does not merely signal the beginning of the reading, but also announces its content. In a world filled with folly, overflowing with lies, distortions, and half-truths, where can we find true wisdom? The deacon announces the presence of wisdom that all may pay attention to it. In doing this, the deacon himself becomes an image of wisdom, saying to all with ears to hear, "To you, O men, I call, / And my voice is to the sons of men. . . . Receive my instruction, and not silver, / And knowledge rather than choice gold" (Prov. 8:4, 10). All too many today place no value on wisdom. They prefer pleasure or convenience. They prefer to have their ears tickled and to hear only what they want to hear (see 2 Tim. 4:3). But in the Church, true and saving wisdom is available, free to all with hungry hearts and the humility to hear.

After this introduction, the reader lifts up his voice to chant the sacred Scriptures as he reads the epistle. As he chants the words of the apostles, we hear not the voice of the reader, but that of the holy apostle himself. The reader should do his best to fade into the words of the text, so that when he reads (for example) the Epistle to the Romans, the faithful encounter not so much the reader with his flowing, sonorous voice as St. Paul, the Apostle to the Gentiles. The epistles are not just historical documents read for archeological interest. They are the living and abiding voice of the Church's first teachers. Though they have passed on, the apostles still speak (compare Heb. 11:4), and through the chanting of the epistle, we still sit at their feet and drink in their authoritative teaching.

After the reader has chanted the epistle, the celebrant blesses him from the altar, rewarding him for his work with a blessing of peace: "Peace be unto you, reader!" In the dialogic spirit of the Liturgy, the reader returns the blessing, saying, "And to your spirit!" and immediately announces the alleluia. As mentioned above, the alleluia is the chanted refrain of the psalm which originally came between the reading of the epistle and the Gospel, though today only a verse or two of this psalm remains. But the alleluia retains its original function of introducing the Gospel with a cry of joy, an anticipatory exclamation of jubilation that we are to hear the words of the Master speaking to us with His living voice. Traditionally, while it is being sung, the deacon censes the Gospel book upon the altar table, honoring Christ in His Gospel before taking the Gospel book in his hands to read it.

It is a dangerous thing to hear the words of the Gospel, for to whom much is given, of him much is required (Luke 12:48). If we hear the truth of Christ, we will be responsible to God for what we do with it. We must not be like the man given a talent by his lord who went and hid it in the ground, doing nothing with it (Matt. 25:18). When we hear the words of the Gospel, we are being entrusted with a treasure, and we must let these words bear fruit in our lives. Otherwise we will hear truth to our condemnation on the Last Day. That is why, before the Gospel is even chanted, the priest prays the Gospel prayer for all who are about to hear it: "Illumine our hearts,

O Master and Lover of mankind, with the pure light of Your divine knowledge. Open the eyes of our mind to the understanding of Your Gospel teachings. Implant also in us the fear of Your blessed commandments, that trampling down all carnal desires, we may enter upon a spiritual manner of living, both thinking and doing such things as are well-pleasing to You."

In this prayer, the celebrant lifts up his voice to God that He may shine His light upon our hearts so that, as we listen to His Gospel, we might know Him better. Understanding the Gospel is not an intellectual exercise, but a spiritual operation. It requires not so much a keen mind as an open and humble heart. We need a fear of God's commandments, a reverence for His Word. "But on this *one* will I look," God says, "On *him who is* poor and of a contrite spirit, / And who trembles at My word" (Is. 66:2). If we listen to Christ's words with a true and trembling heart, eager to learn and accept correction, eager to receive a commandment that we may zealously perform it, then we will indeed listen to our salvation. Then the fruit of our hearing the Gospel chanted will be that "we enter upon a spiritual manner of doing," pleasing God in work and word. We will be not forgetful hearers, but effectual doers (see James 1:25). With so much depending upon our response to hearing the Gospel, no wonder the celebrant first prays for us!

The deacon who reads the Gospel also asks to be prayed for. Standing in the midst of the people, holding the Gospel book and ready to speak, he first asks for a blessing. "Bless, Master," he says to the celebrant, "him who proclaims the good tidings of the holy apostle and evangelist!" If the reader strives to fade into the words of the epistle and stand aside so that the apostle might come forth, how much more does the deacon desire to vanish into the words he is about to proclaim, that Christ our God might come forth! The priestly blessing is given to the deacon: "May God, through the prayers of the holy, glorious, and all-praised apostle and evangelist, enable you to proclaim the glad tidings with great power, to the fulfillment of the Gospel of His beloved Son, our Lord Jesus Christ!" Only after receiving this power does the deacon lift up his voice to proclaim the Gospel of Jesus Christ.

All stand to receive these words, in obedience to the deacon, who directs all to "Stand upright!" The faithful may sit, if they wish, through the long readings of the other Scriptures, resting as they drink in the words of Peter or Paul or readings from the Acts of the Apostles. It is otherwise for the words of the Master—for these words, all stand erect with anticipation, like soldiers standing at attention before their commander.

And even now, after intercession for the people and the blessing for the deacon, after all stand with reverence for the Lord who is about to speak, there is yet one more thing to be done before the proclamation of the eternal words of Christ. The priest once again blesses the people, saying, "Peace be unto all!" which blessing the people return, "And to your spirit!" All the assembly receive the peace and presence of Christ as a final preparation for hearing the Gospel. Only with hearts settled and blessed by God can the faithful fruitfully receive the life-giving words.

Before and after the words are spoken, the faithful greet the living Lord who speaks in His Gospel, crying aloud to Him, "Glory to You, O Lord, glory to You!" Who can measure the importance of these words we are about to hear? No other words spoken in the wide world are like these words from the Gospel. Everything else we hear—all the multitude of words we hear on the news, listen to in movies and television programs, words we take in from coworkers or family or friends, words we read in books and papers—all other words are vanishing dust in the wind compared to these words. Other words may seem for a time to be of lasting weight and abiding importance—news of terrorist attacks and responses, news of wars and rumors of wars. But all this will pass away. Indeed, heaven and earth will pass away—but not these words. As Christ Himself says, His words will outlast the cosmos and will abide forever (Matt. 24:35). As the deacon chants the Gospel, we are listening to something more real than ourselves or the rest of the world around us.

After the Gospel comes an act of daring. After the words of Christ, another will dare to add something! For traditionally, the celebrant preaches the homily after the Gospel. Talk about a hard act to follow! For the task of the preacher is *not* to offer his own views or opinions. His task is to interpret the sacred words just proclaimed, and that is why he preaches immediately after all the readings. If it is a dangerous thing to hear the words of the Gospel, how much more is it to interpret them to the faithful and to speak with credibility and authority, as the voice of the Church? As St. James said, "Let not many of you become teachers," for teachers "shall receive a stricter judgment" (James 3:1). (The Greek for "stricter judgment" is *meizon krima*—sometimes translated "greater condemnation." Here is a text for would-be priests!) Yet, daunting task though it may be, the homily is an essential part of the Divine Liturgy, for the priest is ordained not just to offer the eucharistic sacrifice, but also to teach his flock the Holy Scriptures. For only with transformed hearts made tender by feeding on divine truth can the people take the next step—to advance to the altar of God and receive the life-giving Mysteries.

Chapter 8

The Intercessions

After the Gospel and the homily, the Church offers a series of intercessions as she continues her journey to the Kingdom. The first of these is the **ektenia**, or litany of fervent supplication.

Like many things in the Byzantine tradition, the ektenia has a long history. Originally, it was said as part of penitential processions which were held during times of special need. During times of famine, plague, or other disaster, the Church would go in procession around the city, chanting hymns beseeching God's mercy and intervention. At times the procession would halt and the deacon would read a lesson from the Gospel followed by this special litany. As befitted its penitential character, it included many repetitions of "Lord, have mercy."

The deacon would begin by urging the faithful to pray with special earnestness: "Let us say with all our soul and with all our mind, let us say, 'Lord, have mercy!'" Then after a series of petitions came the final petition of this penitential ektenia, a paraphrase of the great psalm of penitence, Psalm 51: "Have mercy on us, O God, according to Your great mercy," to which the people in the procession would respond with an outpouring of "Lord, have mercy"—sometimes nine or twelve repetitions. (This pattern can still be found in the litya intercessions at Great Vespers.)

Ektenia—
(from the Greek, meaning "fervency, earnestness")—
Originally, a litany or series of prayers offered with special intensity. The term *ektenia* is often now used to describe any litany, not just the litany of fervent supplication.

This ektenia or litany of fervent supplication was very popular, and by the eighth century it had found a place in the regular Liturgy, even apart from special times of crisis. Just as this ektenia was said after the reading of the Gospel when it was part of a penitential procession, so by the eighth century the Church inserted it into the

Liturgy after the reading of the Gospel. As in its former days, it was still characterized by the chanting of many repetitions of "Lord, have mercy," since the people responded to each specific petition with a triple "Lord, have mercy." It was here, in its new location, that it came to be a fixed part of the usual Sunday service.

In our present Divine Liturgy, the litany of fervent supplication functions as a time of especially concentrated prayer. We can see this from the very form this litany takes, for it is different from all other litanies offered in the Liturgy. In the great litany said at the beginning, for example, the deacon's petitions are addressed *to the people*, as he exhorts them to pray for some special need: "For the peace of the whole world, for the stability of the holy churches of God and for the unity of all, let us pray to the Lord." The faithful then respond to this diaconal exhortation by praying to God with the words, "Lord, have mercy." This pattern of diaconal exhortation to the people also occurs in the "litany of asking," said by the deacon before the Lord's Prayer. In that litany, the deacon again addresses the people, inviting them to pray for some specific need—for example, "An angel of peace, a faithful guide, a guardian of our souls and bodies, let us ask of the Lord." The faithful again respond to this invitation, praying to God, "Lord, have mercy."

The litany of fervent supplication, however, is different. In this litany, the deacon does *not* address the people, but cries directly to God Himself, saying after the opening invitations to pray, "Have mercy on us, O God, according to Your great goodness; we pray You, hearken and have mercy!" The people then respond by saying, "Lord, have mercy! Lord, have mercy! Lord, have mercy!" Each petition of the litany is addressed to God directly, and each petition provokes the response of not just a single "Lord, have mercy!" but a triple one. It is as if the people cannot restrain themselves from crying out to God over and over again, begging for His help and laying hold of His boundless compassion. In this litany, the Church stretches herself heavenward, reaching towards God with every fiber of her being. In the early days, when this litany was used outside the Divine Liturgy as an extraordinary intercession during times of special catastrophe, the faithful would take advantage of it to pour out their souls before God. By inserting this litany into the regular Liturgy, the Church commends this fervency to her faithful as part of the norm.

Today we greatly need to recover this sense of urgency in prayer. In our culture, we too often live in a kind of emotional refrigeration. North Americans—perhaps especially those of Northern European descent—are used to refraining from public displays of emotion, and even during times of emotional trauma (such as at funerals), outpourings of grief are not encouraged. We find publicly displayed emotion slightly embarrassing. Christ may have wept openly at the death of a close friend (John 11:35) or at the sight of a hardened and doomed city (Luke 19:41), but we would never lose hold of ourselves in that way—especially in church! It was otherwise in the Eastern Church. The pilgrim Egeria, writing of her travels in the late fourth century, says that in Jerusalem, when the reader chanted the Scriptures describing the betrayal of Christ, "there is such moaning and groaning with weeping from all the people that their moaning can be heard practically as far as the city" (*Egeria's Travels*, ch. 36).

The Scriptures give us little support in our modern North American reserve. The prophet Isaiah condemns those who refuse to stir themselves up to take hold of God (Is. 64:7), and James exhorts the sinfully complacent, "Lament and mourn and weep! Let your laughter be turned to mourning and *your* joy to gloom" (James 4:9). Indeed, some are even told by him to "weep and howl for your miseries that are coming upon *you*" (James 5:1). I do not suggest that our North American liturgical assemblies should become places of unrestrained emotional orgies. We are all culturally conditioned, and it is dangerous to force ourselves unnaturally into other molds. But I do suggest that our intercessory prayer should be more fervent, and that we ought not to fear emotionally fervent prayer. The litany of fervent supplication is a time for the faithful to stir themselves up to take hold of God's help for all the needs of their community and world.

The next intercession that comes in the service books is the litany and prayer for the catechumens. As mentioned before, the catechumens are those inquirers who are being instructed in the Faith as a preparation for Holy Baptism. In the days of St. John Chrysostom, the catechumenate lasted three years or more. During this time, the catechumens would gather together during the Liturgy to be specially prayed for.

The deacon begins by summoning them to attention: "Pray to the Lord, you catechumens!" He then invites the faithful to intercede for them: "Let us, the faithful, pray for the catechumens, that the Lord may have mercy on them!" He then prays for them, asking God to teach them the Word of Truth, to reveal to them the Gospel of righteousness, and to unite them to His Holy Church. At the end of these petitions (to which the faithful respond with "Lord, have mercy!"), the deacon instructs the catechumens to bow their heads to the Lord. They bow their heads for the blessing of the bishop or celebrant, who extends his hand over them and blesses them by saying a special prayer. The bishop or celebrant prays that God will look down upon those catechumens who are bowing their necks before Him, make them worthy in due time of the baptismal washing of rebirth, and thereby number them with His chosen flock. The people say "Amen!" to this prayer. In the early days, the catechumens were then dismissed—and along with them, all the faithful who did not plan to receive Holy Communion.

This litany and prayer have in some places fallen into disuse, since for many centuries the Church had virtually no catechumens. In the early days, the church of the Byzantine Empire had such success in converting people that the only ones being presented for the baptismal "washing of rebirth" were the babies of believers. The litany, where it was retained, became something of an anachronism (and therefore the subject of some very creative—if fanciful—explanations about what it meant).

Today, however, many people would like to enter the Orthodox Church as adult converts and are therefore worthy candidates for a revived catechumenate. Where such earnest inquirers exist, it is appropriate for them to be specially prayed for in this litany. The days of the early Church have returned! For as in those days, the Church now exists in the midst of an unbelieving and often hostile society. We can no longer assume that the country in which we live is authentically Christian. If it ever was, it is so no longer. We now live in a post-Christian culture and need to come to terms with this. The Church increasingly finds itself an island of faith and striving for holiness in the midst of a sea of unbelief and sin. To survive, we need to convert to Christ men and women who have never known Him, and bring them to the obedience of faith. And the historical institution by which the Church carries out this task is the catechumenate.

The catechumenate therefore can have an increasingly crucial function as the Church strives to convert the world afresh. In this context, this litany and prayer can become the focus of the Church's mandate for evangelism, for by summoning the catechumens into one place, praying for them as an identifiable group, and giving them a blessing under the extended hand of the celebrant, the Church is bearing witness visibly to its divinely given task of converting the world. The visible presence of catechumens as a distinct group within the larger congregation serves as a constant weekly reminder to all the faithful that the Church does not exist for itself, but for the world, to bring the men and women God created into a saving relationship with Him. To function as an effective reminder of this task for the faithful, the local catechumenate needs to be prominent and visible.

To have them as a distinct group within the congregation is good; to gather them together and pray for them as a group, blessing them with outstretched hand within the Divine Liturgy, is better. The fathers of the early Church knew what they were doing!

Even apart from this evangelistic role, the renewed emphasis on the catechumenate has another benefit for the assembled Church. It is too easy to devalue the role of the laity, thinking of them as the uninitiated. (This use of the term "layman" is reflected in our very language: one professes ignorance of a subject by saying, "I'm just a layman in these matters.") It is easy to think that the ones who are *really* "in" are the clergy. After all, they are the ones who get to go behind the icon screen. In this way of thinking, the laity are, literally, the outsiders. An active catechumenate reveals to the laity that it is they, the laity, along with their clergy, who are the *in*siders—the ones who have passed through the rites of initiation and are allowed to receive Holy Communion. The catechumens, by being visibly present *as catechumens* without being allowed yet to receive the sacramental Mysteries of the Church, show to the laity the true dignity of their own status. The layman is not the *un*initiated—he is the initiated! Though he may not enter the altar without due cause, he is still the insider, since he has experienced the eucharistic grace of God and knows the Kingdom of God, as it were, from the inside.

The catechumen who has gone through the discipline of the catechumenate and who has waited, week after week, until the time of his chrismation when he may join the laity in receiving the eucharistic gifts *knows* the value of being a layman. He will truly value his status as laity because he has had to wait and prepare for it.

After the litany and prayer for the catechumens in the service books comes the dismissal of the catechumens. The deacon orders the catechumens to depart so that only the faithful remain in the service. This order dates from the days when catechumens were never allowed to attend and see the Eucharist until after they had fulfilled their catechumenate and had been baptized. Since this discipline has long since lapsed (not only do catechumens now know what goes on during the eucharistic part of the Liturgy, but sometimes services are even televised to the public at large), many congregations simply omit this dismissal.

The next prayers in the service books are called "the prayers of the people" because that was the original function of the prayers in this location. But, as we have seen, those intercessory prayers of the people (such as the great litany) have moved to different locations in the service. The prayers that are in this location now are not so much the Church's intercessory prayers *for the world* as the clergy's prayers *for themselves*. They are, in fact, the first clergy prayers of access to the altar. (In some churches, the deacon prays petitions taken from the great litany as a kind of "cover" for these prayers, to give the priests time to say them silently.)

The nature of these prayers as clerical prayers of access to the altar may be seen by examining the text of the prayers themselves. In the first prayer, the priest prays as follows: "We thank You, O Lord God of Hosts, who have accounted us worthy to stand even now before Your holy altar, and to fall down before Your compassion for our sins and for the errors of all Your people. And enable us also, whom You have placed in this Your service, by the power of Your Holy Spirit, blamelessly and without offense, in the pure witness of our conscience, to call upon You at all times and in every place, that hearing us You may be merciful to us according to the multitude of Your great goodness, for unto You are due all glory, honor, and worship, to the Father and to the Son and to the Holy Spirit, now and ever and unto ages of ages."

The second prayer is similar in intention. The text of this prayer is, "Again and oftentimes we fall down before You, O God who love mankind, that looking down upon our petition You would cleanse our souls and bodies from all defilement of flesh and spirit, and grant us to stand blameless and without condemnation before Your holy altar. Grant also to those who pray with us, O God, growth in life and faith and spiritual understanding. Grant them to worship You blamelessly with fear and love, and to partake without condemnation of Your holy Mysteries, and to be accounted worthy of Your heavenly Kingdom, that guarded always by Your might we may ascribe glory unto You: to the Father and to the Son and to the Holy Spirit, now and ever and unto ages of ages."

In both these prayers (the ones from St. Basil's Liturgy have the same purpose), we can see that the priest is praying for himself as a part of his spiritual preparation for approaching the eucharistic altar. The "we" mentioned in the prayers is the clergy; the "they" is the laity praying with them. These prayers have nothing directly to do with the Church's intercession for the world. They have everything to do with the preparation of the clergy.

In this too the Church shows its wisdom. Whether the priest says these prayers silently (the custom in most churches) or aloud, he needs to prepare himself for the daunting task of being God's steward. As another prayer of access (recited silently by the priest while the cherubic hymn is being sung) says, "No one who is bound by the desires and pleasures of the flesh is worthy to approach or draw near or to serve the King of Glory, for to minister to Him is great and awesome even to the heavenly powers." How can the priest, a mere man, one indeed bound by the desires of the flesh as all other men are, dare to approach? Only indeed through the mercy of God. And it is this mercy for which these prayers of access ask.

Chapter 9

The Great Entrance and Prayer of Access

After the intercessions for the world, the catechumens, and the clergy comes the ceremonial bringing in of the gifts of bread and wine in preparation for the eucharistic sacrifice. The bread and wine were previously prepared in a short private service held immediately before the public Liturgy itself. In this short service, sometimes called the *proskomedia*, *prothesis*, or liturgy of preparation, the priest cuts from the available bread a large cube called the Lamb, which will be brought in along with a chalice full of wine and water to be sanctified in the Eucharist as the Body and Blood of Christ.

In Constantinople in former days, the bread and wine were prepared in a separate adjoining building, called in Greek the **skeuophylakion** (or sacristy). In the days of St. John Chrysostom, after the first part of the Liturgy centering on the Scripture readings and the sermon was completed, the deacons would leave the building to go to the adjoining *skeuophylakion*. There they would gather up the prepared bread, the **diskoi**, chalices, wine, and all other items needed for Holy Communion and bring them back into the church temple itself, placing them on the altar.

In St. John Chrysostom's day, the deacons accomplished this procession with a minimum

Skeuophylakion (literally, "vessel guardroom")— In fourth-century Constantinople, a building adjoining the main building of the church containing the vessels needed for the performance of the Liturgy

Diskos (plural, **diskoi**)— A footed plate for the bread of Holy Communion

of ceremony and in silence. It was a purely functional affair, as the deacons went out and brought in the bread, the wine, and the vessels needed for the upcoming eucharistic sacrifice. Meanwhile, the bishop and his priests prepared themselves to offer the sacrifice. They had a brief dialogue, asking that the Holy Spirit aid them in their holy work. They washed their hands, then approached the altar table and said a prayer of access, asking God to "accept the prayer of us sinners and bring us to Your holy altar, enabling us to offer unto You gifts and spiritual sacrifices."

But this purely practical procession did not remain so unadorned. The people knew that they were preparing to "receive the King of all" into themselves in Holy Communion. The preparation for such an awe-inspiring event must surely be made glorious!

Therefore the procession, initially made by the deacons in silence, came to be accompanied by a psalm, probably Psalm 24:7–10. At that time, the Church used this psalm also for the entrance into church when the temple was first dedicated, the psalm being chosen no doubt because of its reference to the doors: "Lift up your heads, O you gates! And be lifted up, you everlasting doors! And the King of glory shall come in."

Its reference to the entrance of the King of Glory made this psalm a natural choice for this eucharistic entry with the bread and wine. The church sang this psalm, together with the refrain "Alleluia!" as a processional hymn every week during the entrance of the deacons with the bread, wine, and other things needed for the Eucharist.

This psalmody, however, did not remain unaccompanied. By the sixth century, another refrain was added, called the cherubic hymn: "Let us who mystically represent the cherubim and who sing the thrice-holy hymn to the life-creating Trinity now lay aside all earthly cares that we may receive the King of all, who comes invisibly upborne by the angelic hosts!" The author of the hymn no doubt intended it to be a theological reflection of the psalm for which it was a refrain—as the "King of glory" entered through the everlasting doors (Ps. 24:7), so Jesus Christ, the King of Glory, was coming to be received as food by the faithful in the Eucharist. In the Liturgy the Church praises God on earth—mystically representing the cherubim, who praise Him in heaven—and joins with the cherubim in singing the thrice-holy hymn to the Trinity, who gives life to both angels and men. Psalm 24, with its cherubic hymn refrain (sung entire, without interruption), was sung by the choir as the deacons brought in the gifts and as the bishop and his priests prepared themselves to receive them.

During this time the faithful waited in anticipation, straining for a sight of the glorious procession. So glorious was the procession that eventually the priests joined it as well. And as the priests passed them, going from the skeuophylakion through the main body of the church into the altar, some of the faithful would sometimes stop them, tugging on the **phelon**, asking to be remembered by them in the upcoming sacrifice. The priests would commemorate them as they passed, saying quietly, "May the Lord God remember you in His Kingdom, always, now and ever and unto ages of ages." Thus would the more pious seek especially to be remembered in the Eucharist.

> **Phelon**
> (or **phelonion**)—
> A long,
> capelike
> vestment
> worn by
> priests over
> their other
> vestments
> during the
> Divine Liturgy
> and other
> services

In the centuries following the seventh century, two other developments occurred in the singing of the great entrance hymn. Firstly, clergy commemorated the people aloud. Originally, as we have seen, the priests in the procession would quietly commemorate the faithful present who asked to be remembered, as the singing went on without interruption. When the emperor attended Liturgy, however, he came to be commemorated aloud. (Being emperor had its privileges!) Eventually, the clergy commemorated others present aloud too, and finally all sorts of people were commemorated aloud even when they were not present.

Secondly, the original Psalm 24 dropped away. Now the entrance hymn consisted simply of the cherubic hymn refrain followed by a triple alleluia.

When these two developments combined, the following situation resulted, which continues to the present day: the choir sang the first half of the entrance refrain (up through "now lay aside all earthly cares"); the priest then commemorated aloud all those he wanted to remember; and the choir concluded by singing the second half of the refrain. Then the priests deposited the gifts on the altar table, and the service continued with the prayer of access.

The prayer of access to the altar (originally said by the priests in the altar area *during* the procession, in the days before they joined in the entrance procession) is now said *after* the procession—since the priests cannot both join in the procession and pray at the altar at the same time. This prayer is the original prayer of priestly preparation to offer the eucharistic sacrifice. It asks that the celebrants may be "made worthy to find grace in God's sight," so that the sacrifice soon to be

Epiclesis (literally, "calling upon") — The invocation of the Holy Spirit during the Divine Liturgy upon the gifts of bread and wine, which transforms them into the Body and Blood of Christ

offered "may be acceptable and that the good Spirit of grace," who is to be invoked at the eucharistic **epiclesis**, "may dwell upon them [the clergy] and upon the gifts lying before" them "and upon all God's people." Today this prayer is preceded by a dismissal litany of asking—that is, a litany originally said for the people before they were dismissed, in which "an angel of peace" and other blessings are asked for those leaving. This litany has no obvious relation to the bringing in of the gifts, and it is sometimes omitted or abbreviated, either here or when it reappears in the service after the anaphora.

This prayer of access, though it has mostly to do with the clergy's preparation to offer the eucharistic gifts, also reveals essential truths about the nature of the Liturgy. For in this prayer, the clergy ask that God's Holy Spirit be poured out upon the whole Church, resting not only upon the gifts of bread and wine, changing them into the Body and Blood of Christ, but upon the clergy and people as well. This prayer reveals the whole Liturgy as an *epiclesis*, an invocation, an appeal that God may transform all present before Him by the outpouring of His Spirit. For it is not just the gifts of bread and wine, brought in at the great entrance and offered at the anaphora, which are changed into the Body and Blood of Christ. We are changed too; we also become the Body of Christ.

The fathers teach without variation: through partaking of the eucharistic gifts, we become what we are. A modern proverb says, "You are what you eat." This is nowhere more true than in the Divine Liturgy, where we become the Body of Christ because we eat the Body of Christ. St. Augustine said so in the fourth century: "The Lord will impart His Body and His Blood which was shed for the remission of sins. If you have received well, you *are* that which you have received" (*Sermon 227*). "It is *your* mystery which is laid on the table of the Lord" (*Sermon 272*). There is an unbreakable sacramental connection between the gifts we offer and ourselves as the offerers of the gifts. For when Christians receive the transformed gifts in Holy Communion, they receive Christ, the King of all. He enters them, transforming them, incorporating them into Himself, so that the assembled multitude becomes again His Body, the fullness of Him who fills all in all (1 Cor. 10:17; Eph. 1:23).

This is why the Church has over the years adorned the great entrance with such splendid ceremonial. This is why the deacon censes the altar, the gifts of bread and wine, and the people prior to the entrance. This is why all manner of liturgical attendants join the procession—not just the deacons, who originally brought in the gifts, but also subdeacons, acolytes, even priests. Each participant in the procession carries some liturgical item in order to make this procession more glorious: the processional cross, the banners, the liturgical fans, the candles.

In our day (when the gifts of bread and wine are kept in the north corner of the altar area rather than outside the church temple, as in the days of St. John Chrysostom), the procession is more ceremonial than practical. Yet we still make this a time of pomp and magnificence and jubilation, and we still make the procession. For in this procession we proclaim that Jesus Christ, the saving Sovereign, the King of kings, the Lord of lords, is coming into our midst in Holy Communion. The adornments celebrate this fact and call us to lay aside all our earthly cares as we approach the eucharistic chalice to receive the King of all. He comes upborne and escorted by the angelic hosts and welcomes us to His heavenly banqueting table. As the Church begins to offer the eucharistic sacrifice (the so-called "Liturgy of the faithful," which only the faithful could attend, as distinct from the "Liturgy of the catechumens," which the catechumens could attend), the Church holds high festival as it brings in the gifts of bread and wine.

Chapter 10

The Peace

After the great entrance, when the gifts have been deposited on the altar table and the clergy have prepared themselves to offer the sacrifice, the deacon says, "Let us love one another," exhorting the Church to exchange the peace. In saying this, it is obvious that he does not simply mean, "Let us have a loving attitude to one another," but rather "Exchange the kiss of peace," for when two or more clergy concelebrate, that is exactly what they do.

The kiss of peace is one of the oldest parts of the Liturgy, going back to apostolic times. In the early centuries, the faithful exchanged the kiss of peace at every Christian *synaxis* (or gathering), immediately after the intercessory prayers. Through this sign of unity and love the Church commended her prayers to God, for such unity and love made her intercession acceptable to Him. In those early times, all Christians gave the kiss to each other, regardless of gender. Each would greet his neighbors standing around him, wishing them the peace of Christ and exchanging the kiss. By the time of St. John Chrysostom (ca. AD 400), men and women stood on opposite sides of the church, and so each exchanged the kiss with those standing on either side, greeting only those of the same gender. Thus, clergy in the altar exchanged the peace with fellow-clergy, men in the nave exchanged it with men, and women with women. But though the logistics had changed to preserve propriety as the Church grew in size and composition, the underlying principle remained the same: the Church still sealed her prayers with the kiss of peace.

It was especially fitting that the kiss should be exchanged during the Divine Liturgy, for in the Liturgy the kiss not only seals the intercessory prayers, but also functions as a preparation for offering the eucharistic sacrifice. The Lord said, "If you bring your gift to the altar, and there remember that your brother has something against you, . . . first be reconciled to your brother, and then come and offer your gift" (Matt. 5:23–24). In the Liturgy, through the kiss, brother finds opportunity to be reconciled to brother, and the Church re-establishes herself in the peace of Christ. For it is only when the Church as a body rests in the peace of God and when all of her members are in unity that her corporate sacrifice can ascend to God and bring salvation to all the faithful. As the deacon today intones, we must first "love one another" (that is, exchange the kiss) and be united in "one mind." Only then can we continue the service and "confess Father, Son, and Holy Spirit, the Trinity one in essence and undivided."

The Church has always recognized and stressed the necessity of being a reconciled and loving community. As early as the *Didache* (a church manual dating from about AD 100), the Church calls her faithful to confess their sins to God and come to Liturgy at peace with God and man: "Let no man having a dispute with his fellow join your assembly until they have been reconciled, that your sacrifice may not be defiled" (*Didache*, ch. 14). We can easily regard the eucharistic sacrifice as something only the clergy do (assisted by the choir or cantor), or we may regard receiving Holy Communion as a private, individual affair (some people even speak of "making my Communion," treating the Eucharist as a private devotion). This is a mistake and a tragic failure to recognize the radically corporate nature of Christian discipleship. No one can live the Christian life in isolation, for each Christian is a member of a body. Even when praying alone at home, we still pray as members of that body, for even there we do not say, "My Father," but rather, "Our Father who art in heaven."

The priest does not offer the Eucharist for the private and personal edification of so many individuals. Rather, through the Eucharist the Church renews her fullness and continually reestablishes local Christians as the united Body of Christ. Obviously, when each Christian receives Holy Communion, he or she is edified, forgiven, transformed, and saved. But this transformation occurs *within the body of the Church as a whole*, and for service in that body. All the people, led by the clergy, offer the Eucharist together. That is why unreconciled conflicts and bitter dissension between local Christians disrupt the peace of the body and (in the words of the *Didache*) defile the sacrifice. It is not that the Eucharist cannot be offered by a quarreling community. It can. But, as St. Paul reminds us, the quarreling members receive the sacramental mysteries not to their salvation, but to their judgment and destruction (1 Cor. 11:17–31).

When we do not fully appreciate the corporate nature of the Church, we fail to appreciate the true significance of the peace as well. If we think of ourselves primarily as individual participants in the Liturgy, it is easy for us to think of the peace as a time for individuals to greet one another *as individuals.* The peace then becomes a kind of liturgical social time, a time to say, "Hello! How are you?" Wonderful as such social exchanges are, they are not what the peace is all about. Such exchanges belong outside the Liturgy at the coffee hour. The peace is not a time to inquire into the welfare of one's neighbor. Nor is it about mutual affirmation, and it ought not to degenerate into a kind of liturgical "hugfest." Rather, in the peace the members of the church acknowledge one another as fellow-members of the same body and each affirms his spiritual solidarity with his neighbor, exchanging the kiss and saying, "Christ is in our midst!" (or, at Pascha, "Christ is risen!"). By greeting only those in our immediate vicinity (that is, about four persons), we can exchange the peace in about ten seconds without disrupting the flow of the service.

In congregations that do not have the practice of actually exchanging the kiss of peace when the deacon tells them to do so, the introduction of the kiss might cause some initial discomfort and embarrassment. We North Americans often have difficulty gracefully incorporating such greetings into such a formal setting as a church service. But that is all the more reason to do so. God means the Church to be a family, and if we hold back from greeting our neighbor because that neighbor is a stranger to us, we have a problem. For how can a fellow-member of the same body be a stranger to us? Congregational reluctance to exchange the kiss thus reveals that the congregation has some growing to do before it can truly be a united family in Christ. Such growing might be painful. But everything alive grows. The only alternative to growth is death. In the Liturgy, God calls us to grow, and Christian growth always involves growth in love.

From the days of the apostles, the Church has affirmed the primacy of love by exchanging the kiss of peace at her services. The restoration of the giving of the peace (where it has lapsed), whether through handshake, hug, or kiss on the cheek, powerfully witnesses to this and manifests the Church as a family, a community which lives and fulfills itself by love.

Chapter 11

The Closing
of the Doors

After everyone has exchanged the peace, the deacon cries out, "The doors! The doors!" as a direction to those guarding the doors to close them and keep them guarded. In this direction we savor the air of the early Church, prior to the peace of Constantine, and we feel ourselves more than ever at one with the Church of the martyrs.

In North America today, we can forget that the most dangerous thing the early Christians did was to celebrate the Liturgy. Every time they did so, they risked their lives. The Roman law made it quite clear: "Christians may not exist," and what defined a Christian, in the eyes of the state as well as of the Church, was participation in the Eucharist. In those first three centuries after Christ, every Christian knew that he or she risked penal servitude, exile, and even death by standing with the clergy at the Christian Eucharist. They never knew when the Roman soldiers would break in on them, gather them up, and lead them away to death. Worshipping the one true God under such a shadow and such pressures left a mark on their liturgical practice, an abiding reminder of the separation of the Church and the world: the closing of the doors.

One of the offices in the church in those days was that of door-keeper. (Canon 24 of the Council of Laodicea in the mid-fourth century mentions this office.) The doorkeeper had the task of standing by the doors and scrutinizing those who entered, making sure that all who entered had a right to do so and excluding all others. When the time came to begin the eucharistic sacrifice itself, he would maintain the security of the assembly by ensuring that no intruders disturbed those who had gathered. For this reason, just before the Church offers the eucharistic prayer (the anaphora), the deacon calls out to the doorkeeper to watch the doors. If the assembly were raided during the Eucharist, the lives of all present would be forfeit. No wonder the deacon tells him loudly (and twice!) to guard the doors!

One may ask, why should we retain such an order today, when persecutions are a thing of the past and when the tramp of Roman boots has long since died away? First of all, persecutions are not a thing of the past. Christians in Eastern Europe experienced them up until the latter half of the twentieth century, and Christians in the Middle East and elsewhere still live and worship under constant threat of arrest and martyrdom. At present, the Church's enemies in North America do not subject Christians to such pressures. But who can tell the future? The elimination of the doorkeeping order as anachronistic might yet prove ironically premature. But even if we do not soon experience a resurgence of persecution in North America, the retention of this call to close the doors reveals something fundamental about the nature of the Church and her worship.

The call to close the doors reveals that Christian worship is essentially a closed, family affair, the private meeting of the heavenly Bridegroom with His earthly Bride far from the eyes of the world. This closing of the doors reveals the separation of the Church from the world, for we Christians no longer belong to this age. Once we belonged to the world, but Christ has chosen us out of the world (John 15:19), and now we live on earth as strangers and exiles. The Eucharist forms our private, corporate communion with our Lord, and the unbelieving world has no part in this communion. As Christ appeared behind the closed and locked doors to commune and meet privately with His own disciples after His Resurrection (John 20:19, 26), so He comes to commune with us in the Divine Liturgy. The unbelievers remain outsiders to this communion. The closed doors form an external barrier and an image of the separation that unbelief makes between the world and Christ. Faith in Christ alone overcomes this barrier. Only through becoming one of the faithful can one stand on the inside, with Christ in His Kingdom.

Chapter 12

The Creed

Having closed the doors, we next recite the Nicene Creed, the symbol of faith. Today we sing the creed as a hymn of praise to the Trinity, a confessional doxology. But the Church hammered out the creed in the smoke of battle—not as a hymn, but as a response to the challenge of heresy, a banner held aloft over the *militia Christi*, a defiant line drawn in the sand, a gauntlet thrown down before those who would dilute and deny the faith of the apostles.

Originally, the Church used creeds only at baptism as part of the candidate's confession of faith. The candidate for baptism would confess his faith in God the Father, who made heaven and earth. He would confess his faith in Jesus Christ, His only Son, our Lord, who was conceived by the Holy Spirit and born of the Virgin Mary, who suffered under Pontius Pilate, was crucified, died, and was buried, who descended to Hades, who rose again from the dead on the third day, who ascended into heaven to sit at the right hand of God the Father, who will come to judge the living and the dead. The candidate would confess his faith in the Holy Spirit, who dwelt in the holy catholic Church, creating the communion of saints and bestowing the forgiveness of sins through baptism, and who would bring the resurrection of the flesh leading to eternal life. Upon this confession of the Church's "rule of faith," the candidate received baptism. If he could not confess this faith, he could not be accepted for baptism nor be a part of the holy catholic Church. Each community used a baptismal creed like this, each identical to the rest in its essentials though differing a bit in the wording. The faith of the Church remained one and the same the world over.

In the early fourth century, a new heresy arose to vex the Church and trouble the unity the Emperor Constantine valued so highly. A presbyter from Alexandria named Arius created a new version of the faith, one that seemed so much more philosophically acceptable and rational than the faith in the threefold God the Church had confessed until that time. As far as Arius was concerned, Jesus Christ was not God—not in any real sense. God was the Father, and the Son was created by God at a certain point (or begotten by Him—Arius used the terms "created" and "begotten" interchangeably), so that before the Father begot the Son, the Son did not exist. The Church had always worshipped the Son as divine along with the Father and the Spirit, but it had never articulated definitively how, while confessing both the Father and the Son as God, the Church could retain a belief in only one God. Arius's notions seemed to many people to preserve the belief in one God by saying that only the Father was God. The Son was, they said, when all was said and done, a creature like everything else. Arius's teaching caught on like wildfire and swept through the Roman world like a raging, roaring disease.

The Church had to deal with this challenge to its faith, and the Emperor Constantine wanted to do all he could to help. He therefore called a council, which eventually met at the town of Nicea in 325, to consider this whole question. It was a momentous occasion. The emperor, as the sponsor of the council, welcomed the assembling bishops, honoring them as the pastors and teachers of the Church. Formerly the emperors had savagely persecuted the Church, but here Constantine shone forth as the first emperor wanting to honor it. Surely, it seemed to all, this could only have come about through the hand of God!

The council fathers considered Arius's statement of faith and overwhelmingly disowned it as foreign to the faith which they had received and which they were teaching to their flocks, for they had proclaimed Jesus as divine and worshipped Him as they worshipped the Father. But how to counter Arius's teaching? For it seemed that Arius and his supporters were able to twist to their own purposes whatever confession the fathers could produce. If the fathers simply confessed Jesus as the Son of God, Arius would agree. "Of course," he would say, "we are *all* sons of God!" It seemed that whatever the scriptural phrase, the Arians (as the supporters of Arius came to be called) proved themselves capable of interpreting it in their own perverse way.

At length the council fathers hit upon a phrase which even the Arians could not twist to their liking: *homoousios*, "of the same essence." And thus the holy fathers of that Nicene Council inserted a number of such phrases into the creed, phrases that the Arians could not confess, phrases they would choke on, phrases that would act as a guard to keep the wolves out of the flock of Christ and exclude the Arians from the communion of the Church. Catechumens had to confess faith in a baptismal creed to become members of the Church: the council fathers put forward a creed that all bishops must confess to remain bishops of the Church. That creed is (with later additions at Constantinople concerning the divinity of the Holy Spirit) the Creed of Nicea.

They were brilliant additions. The creed described Jesus as "light from light, true God from true God." The Scriptures described God the Father as "light" and as "true God" (see 1 John 1:5; 5:20), and the council fathers described Jesus in exactly the same terms, proclaiming Jesus not as an inferior deity, but as equal to the Father in divinity. The creed described Jesus as "begotten, not created"—a stroke of genius, wisdom from God. The Greek word for "created" was *genetos* (with one "n"), while the word for "begotten" was "*gennetos*" (with two "n"s). Arius used the two words interchangeably, thus capitalizing on the similarity and confusion between the two words. The creed here differentiates between these words, admitting Christ was "begotten" by the Father eternally, but insisting that He was "not created"—*gennetos*, not *genetos*. With this phrase, the council fathers struck from Arius's hands one of his best weapons against the truth. The creed describes Jesus as "of one essence [Greek *homoousios*] with the Father," sharing the Father's essence as divine. It describes Him as the One "by whom all things were created," the Creator of all, since the Father created all things through His Word and Son.

All these phrases the fathers inserted into the regular baptismal creed, making it the basis upon which they would recognize in each other the catholic faith. (In 381, at a council in Constantinople, other fathers would add similar expressions to defend the divinity of the Holy Spirit, confessing Him as the Lord, the Life-giver, proceeding from the essence of the Father and not simply created by Him, sharing the worship offered to the Father and the Son, the God who spoke through the Old Testament prophets when they said, "Thus says the Lord.") Here at Nicea, the Church created the creed as a masterpiece, as a way of excluding the poison of heresy from the body of the Church. Any bishop who would not confess this faith the Church anathematized, excluding him from the communion of the catholic Church. Of the fathers assembled at Nicea, 318 confessed this faith. Only two refused and were expelled. The Nicene Creed eventually won the assent of the Church throughout the world, and it became a standard around which the Church continues to rally to this day. By the early sixth century, a patriarch of Constantinople introduced the practice of reciting the creed at the eucharistic Liturgy as a way of proclaiming to all his loyalty to the faith of Nicea. Once it was given a place in the Liturgy, no one who came after wished to remove it lest they be accused of denying the Nicene faith, and so it remains in the Divine Liturgy to this day.

The Arians, the catalysts for the creation of the creed, exist no longer as a faction threatening the Church's unity. Why then does the creed remain in our Liturgy? Surely the Church's adherence to the faith of Nicea no longer needs liturgical support? There are two reasons for retaining the creed in the Liturgy.

Firstly, though Arianism as such is no longer a threat to the Church's unity, heresy remains in the world nonetheless, and the Church must remain forever vigilant against it. The presence of the creed in the Liturgy forms the Church's bulwark against such heresy, for by confessing the creed immediately before praying the eucharistic anaphora, the Church states unequivocally that it is *not* acceptable to believe just anything at all, and that belief is *not* just a private matter. In order to be a part of the body of communicants and remain in the Orthodox Church, one must first share the Church's faith—a faith well-defined and unchanging. Indeed, without this unity of faith, there can be no unity of sacramental communion. For before receiving Holy Communion, all the faithful say the creed together, thus showing that sharing the common faith is a prerequisite to sharing the common sacrament. In our day of pluralism and individualism, we might be tempted to think that any form of belief is adequate, as long as it is sincerely held and uses Christian terminology. As long as we say we believe in Jesus, what does it really matter what we mean by this? Surely individual sincerity is enough?

It is not enough. St. Paul long ago warned us that to be saved, we must have a relationship with the *real* Jesus—the Jesus proclaimed by him and by the Twelve, the One witnessed to by the Law and the Prophets, the One who took flesh and was crucified, buried, and raised (1 Cor. 15:1–8). For a seeker could find other Jesuses on the market, even then. Some people in the first century proclaimed a Jesus who would not forgive anyone who was not a Jew; others proclaimed a Jesus who was not really made flesh, but was a kind of phantom, only *seeming* to be flesh. St. Paul warned us, once and for all, to accept no substitute. Indeed, many in his day preached another Jesus (2 Cor. 11:4) who proclaimed other gospels (Gal. 1:9). These Jesuses were not the true Jesus, and accepting these pseudogospels did not bring one into saving contact with the true Lord. These false versions of Jesus were in fact products of the spirit of antichrist (1 John 4:3) and must be rejected at all costs. Sincerely confessing a Jesus of some sort is not enough, for one can be sincerely wrong. Hitler was sincere. Sincerity alone cannot save us from disaster. Only truth can do that. Retaining the creed in the Liturgy witnesses to the indispensable primacy of the truth. We all want unity, but unity can only be maintained on the basis of the apostolic truth of God. Without this truth, unity is a solidarity of the deceived, a fellowship of the lost.

Secondly, the Church retains the creed in her modern Liturgy because it has become a hymn of praise. In the baptismal service, when the catechumen confesses his faith, the creed is merely *recited;* in the Liturgy as prayed throughout the centuries, it is *sung.* We sing the creed now as a triumphant outpouring of joy, rehearsing the mighty acts of God which He accomplished for us men and for our salvation. In Orthodoxy, theology is primarily doxology, a glorification of God and an offering of praise, not an academic subject; it comes from the heart, pouring from the lips, and a theologian therefore is one who prays and sings. In the creed, the Church, united in the peace of God, lifts up to Him a single confession of faith as a song of adoration. The psalmist declared, "Blessed are the people who have learned to acclaim You!" (Ps. 89:15 LXX). In the creed, the Church acclaims her Lord as she approaches His holy altar.

Chapter 13

The Anaphora

After singing the creed, we take our next step, to the very threshold of the Kingdom. For after the creed, the Church offers the **anaphora**. Once more, the deacon urges the faithful to greater attention. "Let us stand aright!" he cries out. "Let us stand with fear! Let us attend, that we may offer the holy anaphora in peace!" In calling the faithful to offer the holy anaphora, the deacon calls them to an encounter with the living God. No wonder he exhorts them to stand "aright"—in the Greek, *kalos*—to stand well, erect, appropriately, even splendidly, at attention, like soldiers awaiting the arrival of their King. We stand "in fear," with humble hearts, trembling to meet our Lord, who is "borne on the throne of the cherubim, who is the Lord of the seraphim and the King of Israel, who alone is holy and rests among the holy ones" (from the prayer the priest prays for himself prior to the great entrance). Who would not stand in fear before the coming of such a One?

> **Anaphora** (literally "offering")—The long prayer which, said by the priest over the gifts of bread and wine, by God's power transforms them into the Body and Blood of Christ

As St. John Chrysostom himself wrote, at the Eucharist "the priest stands at the altar bringing down, not fire [as Elijah brought down on his sacrifice on Mount Carmel], but the Holy Spirit. And he offers prayer at length, not that some flame lit from above may consume the offerings, but that grace may fall upon the sacrifice through that prayer, set alight the souls of all, and make them appear brighter than silver refined by fire.... Do you not know that no human soul could ever have stood that sacrificial fire, but all would have been utterly annihilated, except for the powerful help of the grace of God?" (*On the Priesthood*, ch. 7). Here is incentive to stand aright and reason to stand in fear. Yet the people do not flinch at this prospect, but reply boldly, looking forward to "Mercy, peace, a sacrifice of praise!" (Scholars tell us that this is the correct way to translate this phrase, reading the first two words in the Greek as two accusatives—"mercy, peace," and not as an accusative and a genitive—"a mercy *of* peace.")

The anaphora is *the* eucharistic prayer of the Church, and the faithful need to hear it. Indeed, the celebrant recited the anaphora aloud until about the beginning of the sixth century, when he began to say parts of it silently. Many regarded this new practice as an unhealthy innovation, and the Emperor Justinian found it necessary to order the clergy of Constantinople to "offer the Divine Offering, not silently, but in a voice audible to the faithful." For the people assemble for this prayer; for the sake of this prayer they offer all the other prayers. In this prayer we offer our sacrifice to God, the only sacrifice we can offer—that of the once-for-all-offered sacrifice of Christ. He is the only true Priest in the Church, for the Church's priesthood has its roots in His heavenly and eternal priesthood. The Church offers the eucharistic sacrifice in that it pleads before God in thanksgiving the eternal sacrifice of Christ on the Cross. As St. Cyprian says, "the Passion [the death of Christ] is the Lord's sacrifice which we offer" (*Epistle* 63). We offer this memorial in obedience to Christ, who at the Last Supper commanded His Church to eat bread and drink wine together "in memory of" Him, as His memorial, His *anamnesis*. By doing this, God "remembers" Christ's sacrifice on the Cross and all that He accomplished for our salvation—that is, He makes it present and powerful in the midst of His people.

Before the anaphora the priest and people exchange a dialogue, blessing and encouraging one another, since both priest and people make this sacred offering. We need this encouragement, for faced with the awe-inspiring approach of God, sensible people might grow fainthearted. We need holy boldness. The celebrant blesses the people with the ancient apostolic blessing (see 2 Cor. 13:14): "The grace of our Lord Jesus Christ, the love of God the Father, and the fellowship [or sharing; Greek *koinonia*] of the Holy Spirit be with you all!" The people return the greeting, "And with your spirit!" The priest then again encourages them, "Let us lift up our hearts!" (Note the first person plural: "*our* hearts," not "*your* hearts," for priest and people make this action as one.) The people respond, "We lift them up to the Lord!" A third time the priest encourages the assembly, "Let us give thanks [Greek *eucharisteo*, from which the term "Eucharist" comes] to the Lord!" They reply, "It is fitting and right to worship the Father, and the Son, and the Holy Spirit, the Trinity, one in essence and undivided!"

Only after this dialogue of mutual encouragement does the priest pray the anaphora itself. This long prayer begins with the words, "It is fitting and right to hymn You," and concludes, "And grant that with one mouth and one heart we may praise Your all-honorable and majestic name: of the Father, and of the Son, and of the Holy Spirit, now and ever and unto ages of ages." Some may not realize this is all one single prayer, since the faithful punctuate it with exclamations. In their joy they cannot restrain themselves from joining in, over and over again. They join the priest in singing the angelic hymn, "Holy! Holy! Holy! Lord of Sabaoth! Heaven and earth are full of Your glory!" They join in by crying, "Amen!" when the priest recites Christ's words with which He instituted the Eucharist. They join in again after the priest says, "offering You Your own of Your own, on behalf of all and for all," as they say, "We praise You! We bless You." They cry out yet again singing the hymn to the Mother of God, "It is truly right to bless you," when the priest commemorates her. It is as if the people cannot contain their enthusiasm, but add their voices at certain points as the priest prays. These insertions, however, should not blind us to the fact that all this is one single, unbroken prayer, and the amen that follows it seals the entire long prayer.

The Church treasures the anaphora of St. John Chrysostom as a liturgical jewel, a concise summary of God's mighty acts. (In Great Lent, the Church uses a different anaphora, that of St. Basil the Great.) The anaphora begins with an ecstatic outpouring. The people have said that "it is fitting and right to worship" the Holy Trinity, and the priest continues that it is indeed "fitting and right—to hymn You, to bless You, to praise You, to give thanks to You, to worship You," not only here at His altar, but "in every place of Your dominion." Words tumble out one after another as the priest stands overwhelmed before the Triune God. He tries vainly to describe such a God, only to find language unequal to the task. "You are God," says the priest, "ineffable, inconceivable, invisible, incomprehensible, ever-existing and eternally the same." We see the difficulty in finding adequate words by the negative adjectives the priest is forced to use: God is *in*effable, *in*conceivable, *in*visible, *in*comprehensible. God's greatness impoverishes our attempts to describe Him; we can more easily say what He is not.

As in all anaphoras (until the third century, the bishop of each community would make up his own anaphora, not using an already fixed text, but rather improvising according to his ability), the celebrant then praises God for all His mighty deeds, both in creating the world and in redeeming it. In the anaphora of St. John Chrysostom, the celebrant uses a great economy of words: "It was You who brought us from nonexistence into being, and when we had fallen away, You raised us up again and did not cease to do all things until You brought us up to heaven and had endowed us with Your Kingdom, which is to come." In these words, the priest praises God for creating us, for calling the patriarchs, for giving the law, for sending angels as guardians, for sending prophets, and especially for sending Christ to save us. In His relentless love for us, God would not rest until He had brought us back to Himself.

For all these manifold and mighty blessings, we now give thanks to the Holy Trinity, "for all things of which we know and of which we know not, whether manifest or unseen." For God continues to pour out blessings ceaselessly upon all the world, mercies past counting, and we would not show ourselves ungrateful for any of them. Especially in that holy hour we are mindful of His great mercy of accepting the Liturgy we then offer Him, and which He "has deigned to accept at our hands, though there stand before Him thousands of archangels and hosts of angels, the cherubim and the seraphim, six-winged, many-eyed, who soar aloft borne on their pinions, singing the triumphant hymn." The people here join in with the priest, singing, "Holy! Holy! Holy! Lord of Sabaoth! Heaven and earth are full of Your glory! Hosanna in the highest." The God of heaven receives the praise of numberless ranks of angels, exalted and transcendent, who soar far above the earthbound creatures with their puny noises. Such a God does not need our praise; He has choirs and songs far better than any we could hope to offer. Yet in His mercy, He deigns to accept our songs anyway and to find our Liturgy acceptable at His throne. How could we not thank Him for this, the crown of all His mercies?

Therefore, along with the hosts of heaven, the blessed powers who sing the thrice-holy hymn, we also "cry aloud" to Him, adding our own echo on earth. The angels cry, "Holy! Holy! Holy!" and we do too: "Holy are You and all-holy, You and Your only-begotten Son and Your Holy Spirit! Holy are You and all-holy, and magnificent is Your glory!"—for He has "loved the world so much that He gave His only-begotten Son, that whoever believes in Him should not perish but have eternal life." Through Christ, the Father reveals His holiness to the world; through Christ, the Father reveals His magnificent glory. Through Christ we are enabled to stand before God and offer Him the same hymn the heavenly angels sing.

With such thanksgivings, the priest then prepares to offer the gifts of bread and wine. In doing so, he rehearses the so-called words of institution, recalling what Christ said "in the night in which He was given up." On that night He "took bread in His holy, pure, and blameless hands, and when He had given thanks and blessed it, and hallowed it and broken it, He gave it to His holy disciples and apostles, saying, 'Take! Eat! This is My Body which is broken for you, for the remission of sins.' And likewise, after supper, He took the cup, saying, 'Drink of it, all of you! This is My Blood of the New Covenant, which is shed for you and for many for the remission of sins.'" The priest does not recite these words as a consecrating formula, as if pronouncing these syllables effected a change in the bread and wine. Rather, the priest speaks these words as his historical authorization by Christ to offer the gifts. The people, for their part, exclaim "Amen!" as they hear Christ's words identifying the bread with His Body and the cup with His Blood. A belief in the real presence of Christ's Body and Blood lives in the heart of every Orthodox believer, causing him or her to cry out in enthusiastic affirmation of this saving truth.

The priest continues with the *anamnesis* (or "memorial"): "Remembering this saving commandment and all those things which have come to pass for us, the Cross, the Tomb, the Resurrection on the third day, the Ascension into heaven, the sitting at the right hand and the second and glorious Coming, and offering You Your own of Your own, on behalf of all and for all"—the people here join in—"we praise You, we bless You, we give thanks to You, O Lord, and we pray to You, O our God!" In this offering of praise, this memorial to God of all Christ has done for us, we come to the heart of our sacrifice. In this sacrifice, we have nothing of our own to offer our God; He has done it all. He owns even the gifts of bread and wine we offer Him, for He has produced them as the Creator, causing grain to grow for bread, causing grapes to ripen for wine. As sinners and debtors to divine grace, we have nothing to offer to God but our praise, our gratitude, thanking Him for all His saving acts, both past and future.

This thanksgiving (Greek *eucharistia*) reveals the essence of Christian faith. As Fr. Alexander Schmemann said in his final sermon, "Everyone capable of thanksgiving is capable of salvation and eternal joy," for Christians find their fundamental calling in thanksgiving. Man is not *homo sapiens*, man of wisdom, created for prideful knowledge, but *homo adorans*, adoring man, for our Creator made us to adore, praise, and bless Him, and any life not built upon the foundation of gratitude to God is not authentic human life. Thanksgiving to God proves that we are truly alive: "The dead do not praise the LORD, / Nor any who go down into silence" (Ps. 115:17). We rightly call the Divine Liturgy "the Eucharist" (thanksgiving), for thanksgiving is the sign of spiritual life, and the Eucharist keeps us alive.

The priest then continues, "Again we offer to You this rational and bloodless worship, and we ask You and pray You and supplicate You: send down Your Holy Spirit upon us and upon these gifts here offered, and make this bread the precious Body of Your Christ, and that which is in this cup, the precious Blood of Your Christ, making the change by Your Holy Spirit, that they may be to those who partake for the purification of soul, for the remission of sins, for the communion of Your Holy Spirit, for the fulfillment of the Kingdom of heaven, for boldness towards You, and not for judgment or condemnation." Once again the faithful cannot contain themselves, but as the priest invokes the Holy Spirit upon the gifts, they cry out, "Amen! Amen! Amen, amen, amen!" (In today's service books, the deacon is the only one to respond with these amens, for when these prayers are said silently, the deacon is the only one of the congregation to hear them. Originally, however, when the priest said the anaphora aloud, all the people said the amens.)

This invocation of the Holy Spirit (the epiclesis, or "calling upon," to use the technical term) expresses the transformative intent of the anaphora. The Church does not effect the transformation of the gifts of bread and wine into the true Body and Blood of Christ by a single formula, but by the entire anaphora. Nonetheless, the anaphora culminates in this invocation. The Church accomplishes the change of the bread and wine into Christ's Body and Blood solely through God's power, and we offer to God Christ's sacrifice by the power of His Spirit. Only through the Spirit, when we partake of the transformed gifts, do we partake for the purification of our souls, for the remission of our sins, for the communion (or sharing in) the Holy Spirit, for the fulfillment in our lives of the Kingdom of heaven, and for boldness towards God. God saves us by this eucharistic eating. For (note carefully) the priest does not simply call down the Holy Spirit upon the gifts of bread and wine, but first and also "upon *us*." We also are "targeted" (as it were) for the descent of the Spirit, so that we may receive these transformed gifts fruitfully and be transformed ourselves. In the anaphora, God pours out His Spirit upon the whole Church, including her offering. And as St. Cyril of Jerusalem (+386) wrote, "whatever comes in contact with the Holy Spirit, this is sanctified and changed" (*Catechetical Lecture* 23). He was speaking about the bread and wine, but his words have other applications. God sanctifies us by this saving contact with the divine; He transforms us by this contact with the Holy One.

Finally, the priest makes a commemoration or intercession for all people everywhere, for Christ died and rose to save the whole world. The priest does not offer the Eucharist as a private benefit for those who happen to be present, but (as the anaphora says) "for all mankind." Here again (as in the great litany) we see the breadth of the Church's generosity, her inclusive spirit, which longs to take up the whole world and offer it to God to bless. It is especially fitting that we make intercessions as part of the anaphora, for (as St. Cyril said in the writing quoted above) "this is the greatest aid to souls, for whom supplication is made while that holy and most dread sacrifice is presented." First of all, the priest commemorates the departed, "those who have fallen asleep in the faith." He includes saints of all kinds, "ancestors, fathers, patriarchs, prophets, apostles, preachers, evangelists, martyrs, confessors, ascetics"—and, as if fearful of leaving out anyone, adds, "and every righteous spirit made perfect in faith." During the commemoration of the departed, the priest offers incense as is customary during prayers and litanies for the dead, swinging the censer as he stands at the altar. This offering of incense shows that God accepts the Church's prayer for the departed (compare Ps. 141:2).

In commending to God the whole body of the Church, he singles out one person in particular: "especially" he commends to God the one who stands at the head of all Christ's saints, "our most holy, most pure, most blessed and glorious lady Theotokos and ever-virgin Mary." In the service books, which presuppose that the priest prays the anaphora silently, the people here break forth in song to the Theotokos, hymning her as more honorable than the cherubim and more glorious beyond compare than the seraphim, magnifying her as truly the Mother of God. In our gratitude to Christ for the salvation of the world, we rightly express our gratitude also to the Theotokos, who with her courageous assent to God and by means of her flesh gave Him to us. Indeed, our gratitude to God is incomplete until it overflows in gratitude to His handmaiden Mary as well. For, as St. Irenaeus said, "What the virgin Eve tied up by unbelief, this the Virgin Mary loosened by faith" (*Against Heresies*, 3,22,4). If Adam therefore could say regarding Eve's disobedience, "The woman gave me, and I ate" (see Gen. 3:12), now we faithful can say of Mary's obedience, "The woman gave me, and I ate," for Mary gave us Christ, whose Flesh and Blood we eat in the holy Eucharist.

All these saints do not stand before God in separation from the other Christian dead whom the Church has not declared saints, nor from the living members of Christ's Church, for all share the same salvation in Christ, and in the Liturgy the Church commends the entire body of the faithful to God. That includes "those who have fallen asleep before us in the hope of resurrection to eternal life," the living members of "all the Orthodox episcopate who rightly teach the word of truth, all the priests, the deacons in Christ, and every order of the clergy." It includes "the whole world," all "the holy, catholic and apostolic Church" spread throughout that world, including those in it "who live in chastity and holiness of life," the monastics hidden from the world's eyes, yet still known to God and included in the bosom of His Church. It also includes "all civil authorities" (who are not necessarily Orthodox Christians), that God may grant them "peaceful times" so that the Church may carry out her mission "in all godliness and sanctity."

The celebrant, if a priest, especially lifts up to God the name of his diocesan bishop, for the bishop is the main celebrant of his diocesan community, and each priest offers the Eucharist only as his delegate. Parishes may think of themselves as self-contained units, but they are not. Rather, each parish lives as part of a larger whole, united to other parishes through the person of the bishop. It is the bishop's Eucharist that all receive, the bishop's faith that they confess. And through him, they share communion with other Orthodox the world over. Elevating the bishop's name at the anaphora reveals these invisible bonds of faith which sacramentally unite the Church throughout the earth.

After praying for the bishop, the celebrant asks God to remember the city in which they live, and every city and countryside surrounding them. He asks God to remember all those in need and danger, such as "travelers by land, by sea, and by air; the sick and the suffering and captives," that they may know deliverance and release. He asks God to remember those Christians who bring offerings for the poor and do good in the churches, and prays that God may send forth His mercies to all. The anaphora comes to its triumphant conclusion as the priest prays that God may grant unity—the same unity bestowed by the Eucharist itself—so that "with one mouth and one heart" all may praise God's "all-honorable and majestic name."

This long intercession (even longer in the anaphora of St. Basil) reveals the nature of the royal priesthood of the Church. Theology defines a priest as someone who offers, and as God's priesthood, we offer His vast entire cosmos back to Him. Nothing in the world escapes God's notice; no tear is shed that He does not catch in His bottle, no pang suffered that He does not note in His book (Ps. 56:8). As a kingdom of priests (Rev. 1:6), we offer our broken world back to Him. He will receive it as an acceptable sacrifice through Christ and will heal it. The eucharistic sacrifice therefore establishes the world and gives it peace. God calls us, as His royal priesthood, to deliver ourselves and our world into His hands, for He is the helper of the helpless, the hope of the hopeless, the savior of the storm-tossed, the haven of the voyager, the physician of the sick.

Chapter 14

The Precommunion Prayers

F ollowing the anaphora and the blessing that follows it, we take a further step towards the Kingdom of God as the deacon intones the litany of asking (so called because of the repeated bidding, "let us ask of the Lord"). Originally the Church used this litany as a series of concluding petitions preceding the final dismissal at Vespers and Matins. Before the deacon dismissed the people, the Church prayed for them that the remainder of their day might be perfect, holy, peaceful, and sinless, and that an angel of peace might accompany them as a faithful guide and guardian of their souls and bodies. The Church prayed that those leaving might leave with the pardon and remissions of their sins, that they might have all things good and profitable for their souls, that they might complete the remaining time of their lives in peace and repentance, and that they might have a Christian ending and a good defense before the dread judgment seat of Christ. By praying these things the Church fortified her members, not sending them back into the world without first asking for protection and blessing from God.

How these petitions found their way into this part of the Liturgy is unclear. Some scholars suggest that by the end of the fourth century, it was common for some who were not planning to receive Holy Communion to leave at this time, and these dismissal petitions were added for them. Whatever their origin in the Liturgy, these petitions were added to an earlier core of other prayers. These earlier petitions ask God to receive our sacrifice upon His holy, heavenly, and ideal altar and to send down in return His divine grace, and to allow us to share in the communion of the Holy Spirit.

The petitions conclude with a precommunion prayer. The text of the prayer is:

To You we commend our whole life and our hope, O Master and Lover of mankind. We ask you and pray You and supplicate You: make us worthy to partake of the heavenly and awesome Mysteries of this sacred and spiritual table with a pure conscience: for remission of sins, for forgiveness of transgressions, for the communion of the Holy Spirit, for the inheritance of the Kingdom of heaven, for boldness towards You, but not for judgment or condemnation.

And make us worthy, O Master, that with boldness and without condemnation, we may dare to call on You, the heavenly God, as Father, and to say:

Our Father, who art in heaven, hallowed be Thy name. Thy Kingdom come, Thy will be done, on earth as it is in heaven. Give us this day our daily bread, and forgive us our trespasses as we forgive those who trespass against us. And lead us not into temptation but deliver us from the evil one, for Thine is the Kingdom and the power and the glory of the Father and of the Son and of the Holy Spirit, now and ever and unto ages of ages.

The people join the priest in saying the Our Father as the conclusion of the precommunion prayer.

The fact that in some places the priest says the beginning of this prayer silently and then prays aloud, "And make us worthy, O Master, that with boldness and without condemnation we may dare to call on You, the heavenly God, as Father and to say," should not make us think that these are two prayers, one said silently and the other aloud, or that the Our Father is yet another prayer. As one can tell by following the sense of the words, we have here one continuous precommunion prayer, beginning with the words, "To You we commend our whole life and our hope," and concluding with the final exclamation of the Our Father, "for Thine is the Kingdom and the power and the glory of the Father and of the Son and of the Holy Spirit, now and ever and unto ages of ages." Thus the Our Father forms the culmination of the prayer. The divinely given Lord's Prayer constitutes, in the service books, the last words on the lips of the faithful as they draw near to receive the holy and life-giving Communion of Christ's Body and Blood.

What better preparation could there be? In Christ, God gives us boldness to dare to invoke Him, the heavenly God, the One exalted far above angels and archangels, who must look far down to observe things not only on earth but also in the heavens (Ps. 113:5, 6). This God, the consuming fire, the One whose face no one can look upon and live (Ex. 33:20; Heb. 12:29), this One and no other we dare to invoke as "our Father," our *Abba* (Gal. 4:6), our Papa. It is His name and honor we long to see sanctified and upheld in the world, His Kingdom and sovereignty we strain towards, His will alone that we wish to have obeyed in this presently rebellious earth. We look for our daily bread to the hand of Him who satisfies each living thing with the food it needs (Ps. 145:15, 16). As we approach His holy altar and draw near to the life-giving chalice, we ask once again that He forgive us our trespasses as we forgive those who trespass against us, that He not bring us into a time of trial (the meaning of the word *peirasmos*, "temptation"), but deliver us from the evil one.

For this is why the Church chose the Our Father as the heart of this precommunion prayer and as our final approach to God. We want to approach with boldness (the word is used twice in this prayer), and we can only have such boldness through Christ's forgiveness. The word translated "boldness" is the Greek *parresia*, often associated with the freedom to speak openly, or (as soldiers sometimes say) "permission to speak freely." One with *parresia* approaches with confidence, sure of being welcomed, free from fear of rejection. Only through this "last-minute" repentance and forgiveness can we have restful hearts and free access to the consuming fire, the Holy One of Israel.

As St. Augustine the Great said, "Why is [the Our Father] recited before receiving the Body and Blood of Christ? Because human fragility is such that perhaps we entertained some improper thought . . . if perhaps such things have happened as a result of this world's temptation and the weakness of human life, it is wiped clean by the Our Father, where it is said, 'Forgive us our trespasses', that we might approach [the Eucharist] safely" (*Sermo Denis* 6). Or, as St. John Chrysostom said, "At the time of the dread Mysteries, we will be able to say with a pure conscience the words of the prayer, 'Forgive us our trespasses as we forgive those who trespass against us'" (*Homily on Ten Thousand Talents*). As we approach the divine chalice, we once again forgive from our heart all who have sinned against us and ask for the forgiveness of our own sins. We draw near not as righteous Pharisees, but as forgiven sinners.

After this comes another blessing by the priest as he turns to the people and greets them, saying, "Peace be unto all!" to which they again respond, "And to your spirit!" The deacon then directs the people, "Let us bow our heads to the Lord!" and the people, with the deacon, bow or incline their heads while the priest invokes God's blessing over them, saying the prayer of the bowing of the heads. As it is often currently practiced, many do not understand the significance of this bowing of heads (especially if the priest joins in and bows his head eastward also). Some suppose it to be merely an act of submission, like a prostration. While there is admittedly a submissive element in this or any act of bowing, we do not bow simply as an expression of inward humility. Rather, the people bow their heads toward the priest *so that he can extend his hand over their heads and bless them.*

This bowing of the heads of all is exactly like the bowing of the heads of the catechumens earlier in the service. The catechumens bowed their heads for a blessing before their dismissal, and here the faithful bow their heads for the same reason. In fact, in the *Apostolic Constitutions* (dated in the late fourth century), the deacon tells the faithful to "bow your heads and receive the blessing." St. Caesarius, writing in about the early sixth century, says, "I admonish you, brethren, that as often as the order is given for you to bow down for the blessing, it not be odious for you to bow your heads, because you do not bow down to man but to God" (*Sermon 73*). The people bow so that the celebrant may extend his hand over the assembly in blessing.

We see this stressed in almost all of the head-bowing prayers, whether in the Liturgy or the daily offices. The full form of our present prayer in the Liturgy says, "Look down from heaven, O Master, upon those who have bowed their heads, *for they have not bowed to flesh and blood* [that is, to the priest], *but to You, the awesome God.*" At Great Vespers, the head-bowing prayer makes the same point: "To You, the awesome Judge who love mankind, have Your servants bowed their heads and bent their necks, *not expecting help from men, but hoping in Your mercy and looking for Your salvation.*" At Matins, the prayer reads, "O holy Lord . . . to You have we bowed the necks of our souls and bodies, entreating You: *stretch forth Your invisible hand* from Your holy dwelling place and bless us all." Some people (as St. Caesarius had evidently discovered) thought it odious and beneath their dignity to bow their heads to the celebrant. But all the prayers show that the faithful, though outwardly bowing to the celebrant and seeking his blessing, ultimately look to God as the source of all blessing and expect the blessing to come from Him. The priest who extends his hand over them in blessing is but God's instrument.

This prayer of the bowing of heads (or "prayer of inclination" as it is sometimes called, from the Greek word for "bow," *klino*) looks towards the dismissal of the people, as did the prayer of bowing at the services of Vespers and Matins. In the Liturgy of St. Basil, for example, this prayer forms part of the precommunion preparation, and it reads in part, "purify us from every defilement . . . so that receiving a portion of Your holy things with a pure conscience we may be united with the holy Body and Blood of Christ." The prayer of bowing at the Presanctified Liturgy is similarly a precommunion prayer.

But not in the Liturgy of St. John Chrysostom, for we find nothing in the prayer, in the original Greek, that speaks of receiving Holy Communion. To some it seems, however, that it *does* mention Holy Communion, for part of the prayer seems to ask that God "distribute these gifts here offered to all of us for our good according to the individual need of each." This, however, is based on the Slavonic text. The original Greek verb (translated from the Slavonic as "distributed") is *exomalizo*, which never means "distribute," but rather "smooth out, smooth away, caress, level out, make even." The phrase should be translated, "*Smooth out what lies before for all of us for good, according to the individual need of each:* sail with those who sail . . ." The prayer asks that God may grant a safe journey to those leaving the church. Some scholars suggest that, like the petitions in the litany of asking that ask for an angel of peace, this bowing prayer also has its origin here in the departure of the noncommunicants who left the church at this point. Whatever the origin of this prayer, it still forms a wonderful part of our precommunion approach to God. For ultimately it is through the Eucharist that the faithful leave with God's blessing. We remain safe in all our journeys because in the Holy Mysteries we have met with the living God, He who directs the paths of all and holds all of us in the palm of His hand.

Then, after quietly praying to Christ that He may have mercy on him, the priest lifts his voice to invite all the faithful to receive Holy Communion. The deacon calls all to holy anticipation, saying, "Let us attend!" and the priest elevates the Body of Christ, summoning the faithful to draw near, saying, "The holy things for the holy!" The faithful cry out in joy, "One is holy! One is the Lord—Jesus Christ, to the glory of God the Father!" We must understand this exchange. The priest is not inviting only the spiritual elite to the Lord's Table, or saying, "If you have been very holy this past week, come to the table and receive the gifts as your reward." By "the holy" ones, the priest means *all the baptized Orthodox Christians there present*. They became holy in their baptism (for which reason the Church calls the sacrament "*Holy* Baptism"), and by this baptismal status they are qualified to come to the altar of God and receive Holy Communion. Baptism made them part of Christ's family, and as His family, the Church summons them to receive His food and to eat at His table.

The eucharistic gifts are "holy," and so are the members of Christ's Church there present. The priest therefore rightly calls the holy people to receive the holy things. We see this more clearly in the Greek—*ta agia tois agiois*—the same word, *agios,* is used, first in the neuter to describe the gifts, then in the masculine to describe the people. The word *agios* is the same word used by St. Paul to describe members of the Church, where it is usually translated "saint" (see 1 Cor. 1:2; 6:1). The faithful are the saints of God (with a small "s," admittedly!), and so the Church bids them to come and receive the sanctified eucharistic gifts. (One could render this phrase as "the sanctified things for the saints.") As Cabasilas says, "The faithful are called saints [holy ones] because of the holy thing of which they partake" (*Commentary,* ch. 36).

Having heard this, the faithful respond with humility. They know the true source of holiness, and so they reply that, properly speaking, only "one is holy," only "one is the Lord"—namely, "Jesus Christ, to the glory of God the Father." Having come face to face with the gift of God, they quickly disown any sense of worthiness or deserving. Without denying the holy status given by the Lord in their baptism, they confess that any holiness they have comes from Jesus Christ, and it is to the glory of God, not to their own glory. In coming to the chalice, they ascribe all glory to God alone.

Chapter 15

The Reception of Holy Communion

t last comes the climax and goal of the Divine Liturgy—
the reception of Holy Communion, when the people of
God step into His Kingdom. Immediately after the
priest invites the faithful to receive and they
respond, as discussed above, the faithful sing the
koinonikon—on most Sundays, Psalm 148:1,
"Praise the Lord from the heavens, praise Him
in the highest! Alleluia! Alleluia! Alleluia!" (There
are other special communion psalms for other
occasions. For example, on the feasts of the Theotokos, the assigned
koinonikon is Psalm 116:13, "I will receive the cup of salvation
and call on the name of the Lord.") Originally, the faithful sang an
entire psalm as the clergy distributed Holy Communion. Thus, in
Constantinople, the cantor sang all of Psalm 148, with the people
singing the koinonikon Ps. 148:1 as the interspersed refrain. As with
all responsorial psalmody, the cantor would chant the psalm a verse
at a time, while the people repeated the refrain after each verse. By
the twelfth century, the psalm itself had dropped away, leaving the
refrain (by then adorned with increasingly complicated melodies) to
be sung by the cantor alone.

> Koinonikon—
> The
> communion
> hymn

In some places, this psalm has been restored. In these places,
after the people sing "One is holy," the choir immediately sings
the koinonikon once (as is done everywhere). They then sing the
koinonikon again as a repeated refrain when it comes time for the
people to receive Holy Communion. The cantor chants the assigned
psalm (for most Sundays, Psalm 148) while the choir responds by
singing the koinonikon refrain after each verse. Thus the chanting of
the psalms forms the background for the sacred act of receiving the

Lord in Communion. We do not receive in silence, but, as in the early Church, with the songs of David echoing in our ears.

The clergy receive Holy Communion first. They receive in the ancient way, putting their right palm over their left and taking the Body of Christ from the palm of the right hand, and then taking three sips of His Blood from the chalice. Even until the days of St. Cyril of Jerusalem (in the late fourth century), everyone used to receive Holy Communion in this way, including the laity. In his lectures to the newly baptized, St. Cyril tells them to "make your left hand a throne for your right, as for that which is about to receive the King. Having hollowed your palm, receive the Body of Christ, saying over it, 'Amen'" (*Catechetical Lectures*, ch. 23).

The practice of the laity receiving both the Body and Blood of Christ together on the spoon did not come in until the eighth century, and its use only gradually spread. Even by the middle of the eleventh century, its use was not universal. Byzantine canonist Theodore Balsamon wrote in the twelfth century that "in some churches" they had abandoned the age-old practice of receiving Communion in the hand—showing that even then the practice of receiving from the spoon was not universal. Scholars have no certainty regarding why the use of the spoon became the preferred method. Some have suggested that the faithful were taking the eucharistic bread home from the service for private and illicit use, and that using the spoon to deliver the gifts directly into the mouths of the faithful ensured they would actually consume it.

Before receiving Holy Communion, the faithful say the communion prayers, "I believe, O Lord, I confess . . ." These were originally said as private devotions (as evidenced by the use of the singular "*I* believe"). Only much later, in the tenth century and after, did they begin to become a fixed part of the public Liturgy. Today, these prayers represent the voice of the people as they stand face to face with the Incarnate God. Here, when we step into His Kingdom and receive the deifying fire into our mortal flesh for the salvation of soul and body, we cannot but confess our unworthiness. We face the Lord Himself and declare our love for Him. Though the world may not believe in Him, we know Him; we believe in Him; we love Him. With St. Peter we confess that He is truly the Christ, the Son of the living God (Matt. 16:16), who came into the world to save sinners. That is why we dare approach Him: He came to save the unworthy; He came to save *us*. We are the sinners He came to gather to Himself. And with a sensitivity to conscience which confounds mathematics, each one present acknowledges himself as "the first" or "chief" of sinners, even as did St. Paul (1 Tim. 1:15).

And not only do we confess Jesus to be the Son of God, we also confess that He is here before us now, present in the sacramental Mysteries. Bread and wine might appear to the sight, but we see with the eyes of faith and confess that this is truly His most pure Body and truly His own precious Blood. The reality of His sacramental presence is not the issue. The issue is the state of our own hearts. Therefore we cry out, "Have mercy upon me and forgive my transgressions, and make me worthy to partake without condemnation. Of Your Mystical Supper, accept me today as a communicant. May the communion of Your holy Mysteries be neither to my judgment nor my condemnation, but to the healing of soul and body." Judas gave Christ a kiss of loyalty and yet afterwards betrayed Him. May we not profess our loyalty with our lips and then betray Him with our lives! In fact, we make no great protestations of loyalty. Rather, we come in abject poverty of spirit, with no merit of our own to plead. Like the penitent thief, we can only beg for undeserved favor: "Remember me, O Lord, in Your Kingdom."

In many places, both the clergy and laity say these communion prayers together, prior to the communion of the clergy. This was the pastoral suggestion of the Orthodox Theological Society in 1980, based on the unbreakable unity of both clergy and laity as the one Body of Christ. The clergy are not divided from the laity in their reception of Holy Communion. Rather, as St. Paul said, "We, *though many*, are one bread *and* one body; for we all partake of that one bread" (1 Cor. 10:17). It is fitting, therefore, that both clergy and laity stand together as one as they penitently approach the throne of grace and pray the communion prayers at the same time.

Whichever way the Church says the communion prayers, either by clergy and laity praying them together or by each praying them separately, the prayers constitute our final cry for the divine mercy as we "draw near with the fear of God and with faith and love." As the chalice is brought out to the people, they acknowledge Christ's sacramental presence, singing, "Blessed is He that comes in the name of the Lord [compare Matt. 23:39]! God is the Lord and has revealed Himself to us!" As Cabasilas says, "The faithful adore and bless the divinity of Jesus under the sacramental veils" (*Commentary*, ch. 39). As Christ came to Jerusalem and was acclaimed by those there, even so He comes to us now through the chalice, and we also acclaim His saving presence. The faithful come to receive the Lord Christ and the Kingdom of Heaven. God has said, "Open your mouth wide, and I will fill it" (Ps. 81:10). Through the Eucharist, God indeed fills us with His love. And having received our Lord, our hearts and mouths are filled with His praise.

The question is sometimes asked, "How often should one receive Holy Communion?" The many aspects of this question put it somewhat beyond the scope of the present volume. But we must give due weight to the voices of the fathers in Christian antiquity. In the days of, for example, St. Cyprian of Carthage (+258), not just weekly, but daily Communion was the norm. He writes, "[In the Lord's Prayer, the words 'Give us this day our daily bread'] may be taken either spiritually or literally. . . . We ask that this bread be given us daily, lest we, who live in Christ and receive the Eucharist every day as the food of salvation, be separated from His Body by some grave sin that keeps us from Communion and so deprives us of our heavenly bread" (*Treatise on the Lord's Prayer*, ch. 18). St. Basil the Great (+379) also knew of such frequent Communion. He writes, "Daily Communion and participation in the holy Body and Blood of Christ is a good, helpful practice. . . . For myself, I communicate four times a week: on the Lord's Day, on Wednesday, on Friday and Saturday, and on the other days if there is a commemoration of a martyr" (*Epistle 93*).

St. John Chrysostom knew of the practice of attending the Liturgy without partaking—and condemned it. In his sermon to his flock, he asked them rhetorically, "Why stay and yet not partake of the Table? 'I am unworthy' you will say. Then you are also unworthy of the communion you have had in the prayers! For it is not by means of the offerings only, but also by means of those songs, that the Spirit descends all around. So that I may not then be the means of increasing your condemnation, I entreat you not to forbear coming, but to render yourselves worthy both of being present and of approaching" (*Homily 3 on Ephesians*). It would seem then the fathers would find the practice of infrequent Communion alien to their mindset. When the deacon summons us, saying, "In the fear of God and with faith and love," we should indeed draw near. The litany and prayer of thanksgiving offered at the end ("We thank You, O Master, that You have made us worthy this day of Your heavenly and immortal Mysteries") presupposes that those listening to the prayer have done just that.

Chapter 16

The Final Rites

After all have received from the life-giving cup of salvation, the Church accomplishes the final rites very quickly. The priest gives a final blessing to the people with the chalice (or, in some churches, with his hand), saying, "O God, save Your people and bless Your inheritance." The people then sing the **stich** "We have seen the true light," which the Church also sings at the Great Vespers of Pentecost. We rightly sing this hymn of Pentecost at the Liturgy, for it was at the first Pentecost that Christ poured out the Spirit upon His Church, and in the Eucharist He again pours out the Spirit upon us.

> **Stich**
> (or **stichos**)—
> A short liturgical hymn

This hymn reveals Christian experience as one *of fulfillment:* in Christ, God fulfills everything, He gives everything to us, and nothing remains to be done that is not done. We have seen the true Light and have been enlightened. We have received the heavenly Spirit and have been brought to heaven. We have found the true Faith and have been brought into the saving presence of the undivided Trinity. What more remains to be done? Through the Eucharist, Christ has accomplished everything for us.

After this, the priest lifts up the chalice before the people one last time, saying, "Always, now and ever, and unto ages of ages." Originally, these words were but the end of the doxological ascription of praise following the *koinonikon* psalm sung during Communion. The passage of time saw changes to these things, and the psalm itself dropped out, leaving the words, "always, now and ever and unto ages of ages" dangling in midair, part of a doxology with no psalm for which it was meant to be the conclusion. Later on, some added the words "Blessed is our God" to the beginning, turning it from a meaningless clause into a blessing. In the Liturgy, everything has a function—even if it is not the original one! During this final blessing, the deacon transfers the gifts from the altar to the **table of oblation.**

Table of oblation—
The table placed in the northeast corner of the altar area where the gifts of bread and wine are prepared before the Liturgy

While the deacon accomplishes the transfer, we sing the hymn, "Let our mouths be filled with Your praise, O Lord." This hymn is very ancient. In the year 624, Patriarch Sergius of Constantinople added it to the end of the *koinonikon* psalm that the people sang during the distribution of Holy Communion, and this hymn has retained a place in the Liturgy even now, after it has been separated from the *koinonikon*. We still delight to sing this hymn, for we long that our mouths, which have been filled with the Body and Blood of Christ, may continue to be filled with His praise. In this prayer we ask that the experience of joy we receive at the chalice may continue with us as we depart, and may sustain us as we walk in His holiness. Having received His holy and life-creating Mysteries, we do not instantly return to the same mediocre life we knew before. Instead, having been inwardly transfigured, we long to remain with our Lord for as long as possible, meditating on His righteousness, singing of His glory. Like the apostles on the Mount of Transfiguration, we cry out, "Lord, it is good to be here!" (Matt. 17:4). We have basked in His light and are reluctant to leave.

After this, the deacon offers the litany of thanksgiving (an expanded version of the original "Let us pray to the Lord" by which he introduced all prayers in the days of St. John Chrysostom). The celebrant then concludes with a thanksgiving prayer offered for all present. In this prayer he gives thanks to God that He has made us worthy of His heavenly and immortal Mysteries (note the assumption that all present have received Holy Communion) and he prays that God might continue to strengthen and guard them through the prayers of the glorious Theotokos and of all His saints. Through the Eucharist God has made us bold with holy boldness, and we leave the Liturgy fearlessly, trusting in His care: our path lies straight before us; God strengthens and guards us, making our steps firm. Though the wicked flee when no one pursues them, through Christ and His saints the righteous are bold as a lion (compare Prov. 28:1).

The deacon then bids all "depart in peace," and the priest leaves the altar to offer the prayer before the ambo. Here we must ask the question, "What is (or was) an ambo?" The word "ambo" today refers to the raised part of the platform in front of the royal doors, where the priest stands to give sermons. Originally, however, in the days of St. John Chrysostom, the ambo was an impressive piece of furniture standing in about the middle of the nave, a raised platform enclosed by a parapet and accessed by a short flight of steps at both the front and the back, rather like a pulpit with stairs. It was connected to the altar area by a raised walkway called a *solea*, so that clergy had unhindered access to the altar in a crowded church. The readers would read the lessons from the top of the ambo. St. John Chrysostom used to preach from there.

In those days, when the clergy left the church after the service, they would leave via the *solea* and the ambo, walking down the *solea* to the ambo and from there out of the church. From the end of the eighth century onwards, the celebrant would stop on his way out and say a final prayer for the people as they dispersed—what is now "the prayer before the ambo." The priest did not offer this prayer publicly, as a part of the Liturgy itself, but as his private pastoral devotion for his flock. The Church used quite a number of these ambo prayers, since each feast had its own special prayer (some forty have survived). These variable prayers continued in use until quite late, only being replaced by a single unvaried prayer (our present ambo prayer) in the fourteenth century. Even now that the piece of furniture called the ambo has vanished from our churches, the priest still goes out to where it once stood (old habits die hard!), leaving the altar to pray for the flock in the words of a prayer once known as "the seal of all the prayers."

In its present form, this prayer indeed sums up all our intercessions. The priest, looking one last time at his people with a pastor's heart, asks that God might save and bless them, that He might sanctify those who love the beauty of His house and glorify them in return for their love with His divine power, never forsaking the little flock who put all their hope in Him. Not only does the priest pray for his own people as they prepare to depart, he also prays for the whole world to which they will return. He asks God to give peace to His world, to all His churches and clergy, to all the civil authorities. God delights to give gifts (compare James 1:17)—may He continue to give these good gifts to His world.

After this prayer (unlike in the eighth century and later, when he prayed this prayer on his way out), the priest now returns to the altar. That is because other elements have been added to the end of the Liturgy. For next comes the triple chanting of Ps. 113:2, "Blessed be the name of the Lord, henceforth and forevermore!" and the blessing, "The blessing of the Lord be upon you," along with the dismissal.

(All these are borrowed from the services of **Typika** and the **Divine Office**, for there was an increasing tendency to end all the services the same way.) These additions, of course, prolonged the true ending of the service. It is as if the Church cannot bear to leave the Lord's presence.

The service ends therefore with all giving glory to God. As the priest cries out, "Glory to You, O Christ our God and our hope, glory to You!" the people reply by giving glory to the Trinity, and the priest steps forward lifting high over them the holy cross. Holding it aloft, he asks that Christ our true God may have mercy upon us and save us. For we do not come to Christ alone, but as part of a mighty and heavenly multitude. We ask His mercy through the prayers of His most pure Mother, of the holy apostles, of St. John Chrysostom, of the patron of the local church community, of the holy and righteous ancestors of God, Joachim and Anna, of the saints especially commemorated that day, and indeed, of all the saints.

The Divine Liturgy is therefore not just the prayer service of a few people assembled in a given place, but our participation on earth in the eternal outpouring of praise thundering joyously in heaven. In the Liturgy, God lifts us up to the Kingdom and makes us sit with Christ in the heavenly places (Eph. 2:6). The Liturgy is our journey, begun on earth but ending in the Kingdom. For in it, God gives the Kingdom of heaven to the children of men.

Conclusion

Living as the Light of the World

At the end, we may ask, what is it all for? What is the ultimate purpose of all these prayers, and of the Eucharist itself? In answer, we may relate the story of a few monks who were discussing which part of the Liturgy was the most important. "The reading of the Gospel," said one monk, "for in it the words of our Savior Christ come to us." "The reception of Holy Communion," said another, "for that is where we receive the very life of God." Finally the third spoke. "Forgive me, brothers," he said, "but I think that the dismissal at the end is the most important. For that is when we leave the church to go into the world and strive to live out the words of Christ with the life and strength He gives us."

And so it is. For God has not made the Liturgy an end in itself, any more than He has made the salvation of our souls an end in itself. Rather, we are saved to serve. In the Divine Liturgy, God glorifies us so that we may bring others to that experience of glory as well. Christ claimed to be the Light of the world (John 8:12). And, even more extraordinary, He claimed that we, His disciples, were the light of the world (Matt. 5:14), for He calls us to partake of His divine nature (2 Pet. 1:4), to experience by grace what He is in Himself. Christ, the eternal Light of the Father, shines in this darkened age, and without Him, all live in the moonless night of ignorance, sin, and death (John 12:46). In the Liturgy, Christ fills us with Himself, with His light, His life, His holiness. Then He sends us back out into the world that our light may so shine before men, that they too might glorify our Father in heaven. The final goal of the Liturgy is nothing less than the transfiguration and illumination of the world.

This will not finally be accomplished until Christ's second and glorious Coming, for which reason St. Paul said that in the Eucharist we proclaim the Lord's death until He comes (1 Cor. 11:26). In this age, we live not by sight, but by faith, including faith in the sacramental Mysteries. Here we see the Lord only under the veils of bread and wine; only after He returns in glory shall we see Him face to face. One day—may God hasten it!—the Kingdom for which we pray daily will come, and the earth will be full of the knowledge of the Lord as the waters cover the sea (Is. 11:9). Then the earth will no longer have any need of sun or moon to shine upon it, for the glory of God will illumine it, and the nations will walk by its light (Rev. 21:23–24).

In that day, all sacramental signs will be no more, for the reality they signify will fill the world. Then we will no longer be dismissed from the Lord's presence, but will remain before Him. We will see His face, and He will illumine us, and we will reign forever (Rev. 22:4–5). As Christ promised, in that day, we will shine like the sun in the Kingdom of our Father (Matt. 13:43). In the Divine Liturgy, we even now take our weekly journey to that Kingdom.

Appendix

A Comparative Chart of Liturgical Development

The Liturgy in the time of St. Justin Martyr, ca. AD 150

- Bishop greets the faithful, "Peace be to all!"; they respond, "And to your spirit!"

- Three readings: Old Testament lesson; psalm chanted with refrain; epistle; psalm chanted with "alleluia" refrain; Gospel reading

- Sermon

- Litany and intercessory prayers of the faithful

- Kiss of peace

- Gifts placed on altar

- Anaphora (said aloud)

- Breaking of bread, "The holy things for the holy!"; Communion received in the hand

- Dismissal: "Depart in peace!"

The Liturgy in the time of St. John Chrysostom, ca. AD 400

- Entrance prayer offered by clergy at the doors to the nave after faithful have assembled with them in the **narthex**

- Entry of clergy into the nave and up into the altar (in silence), preceded by candles and incense; deacon carries Gospel and places it on altar table

> **Narthex—**
> The large vestibule leading to the *nave*

- Bishop goes to his chair at the high place; greets the faithful, "Peace be to all!"; they respond, "And to your spirit!"
- Three readings: Old Testament lesson; psalm chanted with refrain; epistle; psalm chanted with "alleluia" refrain; Gospel reading
- Sermon
- Litany and prayer for catechumens
- Dismissal of catechumens
- Closing of doors
- Great litany (intercessory prayers of the faithful)
- Kiss of peace
- Transfer of gifts from skeuophylakion to altar (in silence) while clergy offer prayer of access to altar
- Anaphora (said aloud)
- Breaking of bread, "The holy things for the holy!"; Communion received in the hand
- Dismissal: "Depart in peace!"

The modern shape of the Liturgy, from ca. AD 1300

- Clergy enter altar to prepare bread and wine at table of oblation before faithful have assembled
- Opening benediction, "Blessed is the Kingdom"
- Great litany and prayer
- Three antiphons and their prayers
- Entrance prayer for entrance back into altar
- Little entrance with Gospel (going from altar area, through nave, back into altar area)
- Troparia/hymns of day
- Trisagion prayer and trisagion hymn
- Celebrant greets the faithful, "Peace be to all!"; they respond, "And to your spirit!"
- Two readings: one verse of psalm chanted with refrain; epistle;

two verses of psalm chanted with "alleluia" refrain; Gospel reading

- Sermon
- Litany of fervent supplication and prayer
- Litany of catechumens and prayer of catechumens
- Dismissal of catechumens
- Litany and two prayers of clergy access to altar
- Transfer of gifts from table of oblation in altar area through nave to altar table, with singing of cherubic hymn, making commemorations in midst of hymn
- Litany of asking with prayer of access to altar
- "The doors, the doors!"
- Kiss of peace
- The creed
- Anaphora (said silently)
- Litany of asking, with precommunion prayer and the Our Father
- Breaking of bread, "The holy things for the holy!"; Communion received from the spoon
- Thanksgiving litany and prayer
- Dismissal: "Depart in peace!"
- Prayer before ambo
- "Blessed be the name of the Lord henceforth and forevermore!" and dismissal (from the Daily Office)

Index to terms defined in boxes:

Also by Father Lawrence Farley:

The Orthodox Bible Study Companion series:

This commentary series was written for the average layperson, for the nonprofessional who feels a bit intimidated by the presence of copious footnotes, long bibliographies, and all those other things which so enrich the lives of academics. Working from a literal translation of the original Greek, this commentary examines the text section by section, explaining its meaning in everyday language. Written from an Orthodox and patristic perspective, it maintains a balance between the devotional and the exegetical, feeding both the heart and the mind.

The Gospel of Matthew: Torah for the Church
• Paperback, 392 pages (ISBN 978-0-9822770-7-2)

The Gospel of Mark: The Suffering Servant
• Paperback, 280 pages (ISBN 978-1-888212-54-9)

The Gospel of Luke: Good News for the Poor
• Paperback, 432 pages (ISBN 978-1-936270-12-5)

The Gospel of John: Beholding the Glory
• Paperback, 376 pages (ISBN 978-1-888212-55-6)

The Acts of the Apostles: Spreading the Word
• Paperback, 352 pages (ISBN 978-1-936270-62-0)

The Epistle to the Romans: A Gospel for All
• Paperback, 208 pages (ISBN 978-1-888212-51-8)

First and Second Corinthians: Straight from the Heart
• Paperback, 319 pages (ISBN 978-1-888212-53-2)

Words of Fire: The Early Epistles of St. Paul to the Thessalonians and the Galatians
• Paperback, 172 pages (ISBN 978-1-936270-02-6)

The Prison Epistles: Philippians – Ephesians – Colossians – Philemon
• Paperback, 224 pages (ISBN 978-1-888212-52-5)

Shepherding the Flock: The Pastoral Epistles of St. Paul the Apostle to Timothy and Titus
• Paperback, 144 pages (ISBN 978-1-888212-56-3)

The Epistle to the Hebrews: High Priest in Heaven
• Paperback, 184 pages (ISBN 978-1-936270-74-3)

Universal Truth: The Catholic Epistles of James, Peter, Jude, and John
• Paperback, 232 pages (ISBN 978-1-888212-60-0)

The Apocalypse of St. John: A Revelation of Love and Power
• Paperback, 240 pages (ISBN 978-1-936270-40-8)

The Christian Old Testament: Looking at the Hebrew Scriptures through Christian Eyes

Many Christians see the Old Testament as "the other Testament": a source of exciting stories to tell the kids, but not very relevant to the Christian life. *The Christian Old Testament* reveals the Hebrew Scriptures as the essential context of Christianity, as well as a many-layered revelation of Christ Himself. Follow along as Fr. Lawrence Farley explores the Christian significance of every book of the Old Testament.
• Paperback, 160 pages (ISBN 978-1-936270-53-8)

The Empty Throne: Reflections on the History and Future of the Orthodox Episcopacy

In contemporary North America, the bishop's throne in the local parish stands empty for most of the year. The bishop is an honored occasional guest rather than a true pastor of the local flock. But it was not always so, nor need it be so forever. Fr. Lawrence Farley explores how the Orthodox episcopacy developed over the centuries and suggests what can be done in modern times to bring the bishop back into closer contact with his flock.
• Paperback, 152 pages (ISBN 978-1-936270-61-3)

Following Egeria: A Visit to the Holy Land through Time and Space

In the fourth century, a nun named Egeria traveled through the Holy Land and wrote an account of her experiences. In the twenty-first century, Fr. Lawrence Farley followed partially in her footsteps and wrote his own account of how he experienced the holy sites as they are today. Whether you're planning your own pilgrimage or want to read about places you may never go, his account will inform and inspire you.
• Paperback, 160 pages (ISBN 978-1-936270-21-7)

Note: To obtain current ordering information, or to place a credit card order, please call Ancient Faith Publishing at (800) 967-7377 or (219) 728-2216, or log on to our website: store.ancientfaith.com.

Introductory book on the Orthodox Church:

WHAT IS THE ORTHODOX CHURCH?
by Father Marc Dunaway (Published by Ancient Faith Publishing)
A brief overview of Orthodoxy. Outlines the history of the Christian Church, with concise explanations and helpful "at-a-glance" timelines. Includes the Age of Persecution, the Age of Councils, the Great Schism, the Protestant Reformation, and more.

THE ORTHODOX CHURCH
By Bishop Kallistos Ware (Published by Penguin)
This classic introductory work on the Orthodox Church has become a worldwide standard in colleges and seminaries. Part One describes the history of the Orthodox Church. Part Two outlines Orthodox doctrine and worship. The final chapter deals with restoring the breaches between East and West.

INTRODUCING THE ORTHODOX CHURCH
By Father Anthony Coniaris (Published by Light & Life)
Fr. Coniaris provides his readers with an invaluable introduction to the beliefs, practices, and patterns of Orthodox Christianity. Written in a popular and easy-to-read style, Introducing the Orthodox Church touches all the important bases without sacrificing balance or accuracy.

THE ORTHODOX FAITH (4 volumes)
By Father Thomas Hopko (Published by Orthodox Christian Publication Center)
An introductory handbook on Orthodox faith and life. Volume 1: Doctrine; Volume 2: Worship; Volume 3: Bible and Church History; Volume 4: Spirituality. Presented in brief chapters, this handbook series is excellent for quick reference or study, and provides valuable teaching material for both teens and adults.

THIRSTING FOR GOD
By Matthew Gallatin (Published by Ancient Faith Publishing)
In Thirsting for God, philosophy professor Gallatin expresses many of the struggles that a Protestant will encounter in coming face to face with Orthodoxy: such things as Protestant relativism, rationalism versus the Orthodox sacramental path to God, and the unity of Scripture and Tradition. He also discusses praying with icons, praying written prayers, and many other Orthodox traditions. An outstanding book that will give Protestant readers a more thorough understanding of the Church.

BECOMING ORTHODOX
By Father Peter Gillquist (Published by Ancient Faith Publishing)
The inspiring story of over two thousand evangelical Christians and their search for historic Christianity. This book is for evangelical Christians on their own search for the Church. It is also for Orthodox Christians looking for renewal.

THE ORTHODOX WAY
By Bishop Kallistos Ware (Published by St. Vladimir's Seminary Press)
An excellent companion to The Orthodox Church, this book discusses the spiritual life of the Christian, and sets forth the basic issues of theology, but as a way of life for the follower of Christ.

To request a catalog, to obtain current pricing or ordering information, or to place a credit card order, please call Ancient Faith Publishing at (800) 967-7377 or (219)728-2216, or log on to our website: store.ancientfaith.com

Ancient Faith Publishing hopes you have enjoyed and benefited from this book. The proceeds from the sales of our books only partially cover the costs of operating our nonprofit ministry—which includes both the work of **Ancient Faith Publishing** and the work of **Ancient Faith Radio.** Your financial support makes it possible to continue this ministry both in print and online. Donations are tax-deductible and can be made at **www.ancientfaith.com.**

To request a catalog of other publications,
please call us at (800) 967-7377 or (219) 728-2216
or log onto our website: **store.ancientfaith.com**

*Bringing you Orthodox Christian music, readings,
prayers, teaching, and podcasts 24 hours a day since 2004 at*
www.ancientfaith.com

CPSIA information can be obtained
at www.ICGtesting.com
Printed in the USA
FFOW02n1148210417
34740FF